ATHLETICS

How to become a Champion

A discursive textbook

PERCY WELLS CERUTTY

Olympic Coach — Australia
10 January 1895 – 14 August 1975

A Classic Revival from

www.pmabooks.com

This book first published April 1960
by Stanley Paul & Co Ltd, London W1

This edition published 2013 by
PMA Books, Classic Revival Series
Brisbane, Australia
with the kind permission of the
Percy Cerutty Estate

Original photographs by
M. A. STRATTON
Melbourne

A Classic Revival from

www.pmabooks.com
PO Box 5197, Manly Qld 4179 AUSTRALIA
Tel + 61 488 224 929 * m. 0488 224 929

PUBLISHING DIRECTOR: Judy Hinz
email judyhinz@pmabooks.com

Publisher's Foreword

My name is Peter Masters. During the summer school holidays of 1964/65, as a 16 year old, I spent around two weeks at Percy Cerutty's athletics camp at Portsea in Victoria, Australia.

I'd become interested in athletics during my schooldays. I had some success as a middle distance runner and having read *The Golden Mile* by Herb Elliott with Alan Trengrove, I was inspired by his achievements, although I was realistic in that I didn't think I possessed talent of that calibre.

Back in the early 1960s, the only way to contact someone was by letter, so I wrote to Percy Cerutty asking if I could come to Portsea to train with him. I set out my modest achievements in making a schoolboy final of the 880 yards (800 metres).

I received a reply from his wife Nancy. It was a friendly letter enclosing the application form and a schedule of fees.

I was thrilled to receive the letter but I was also concerned at how I would afford to attend Portsea. I came from a family of seven children (all boys) and there was certainly no extra money to send me from my home in Sydney to Portsea in Victoria to train with Percy Cerutty.

However, that didn't stop me. I got an after school job selling the afternoon newspapers on the corner of Pitt and Market Streets in the city of Sydney. Afternoon papers were in great demand in those days. So that was how I earned the money to pay for my time at Portsea.

What do I remember about Portsea and about Percy?

First impressions: a madman!

Well not really but I'd never met anyone like him before. He was scary to a 16 year old, but compelling. He had a larger than life persona.

I remember it was hot at Portsea which made training even more arduous.

I remember too that there were some very talented older athletes, so I felt a bit over-awed.

Percy's methods were unconventional and sometimes seemed a bit extreme such as his exaggerated running action, which he used really to make a point.

I remember training up the sandhills.

One day, a boy blacked out in front of me and tumbled down the sandhill and when I went to his aid, Percy yelled out words to the effect that 'he's not dead so don't stop'.

The boy recovered of course but the incident illustrated Percy's determination.

I remember one day we headed to the beach to train and of course moved to below the high water mark to run on the hard sand.

Once again we heard a booming voice telling us to run in the soft sand. There were never any easy options.

The original copy of this book, which has been with me since 1964, has proved an inspiration throughout my life.

I didn't go on to become a champion athlete but I admired Percy Cerutty for his willingness to 'push the boundaries' and to challenge accepted practice.

I think Percy's philosophies are as relevant today as they were back in my youth.

It is for that reason that I wanted to bring Percy's books to a new audience.

I hope you gain as much inspiration from his ideas as I did.

Good running.

Peter Masters
PMA Books
Brisbane, Australia

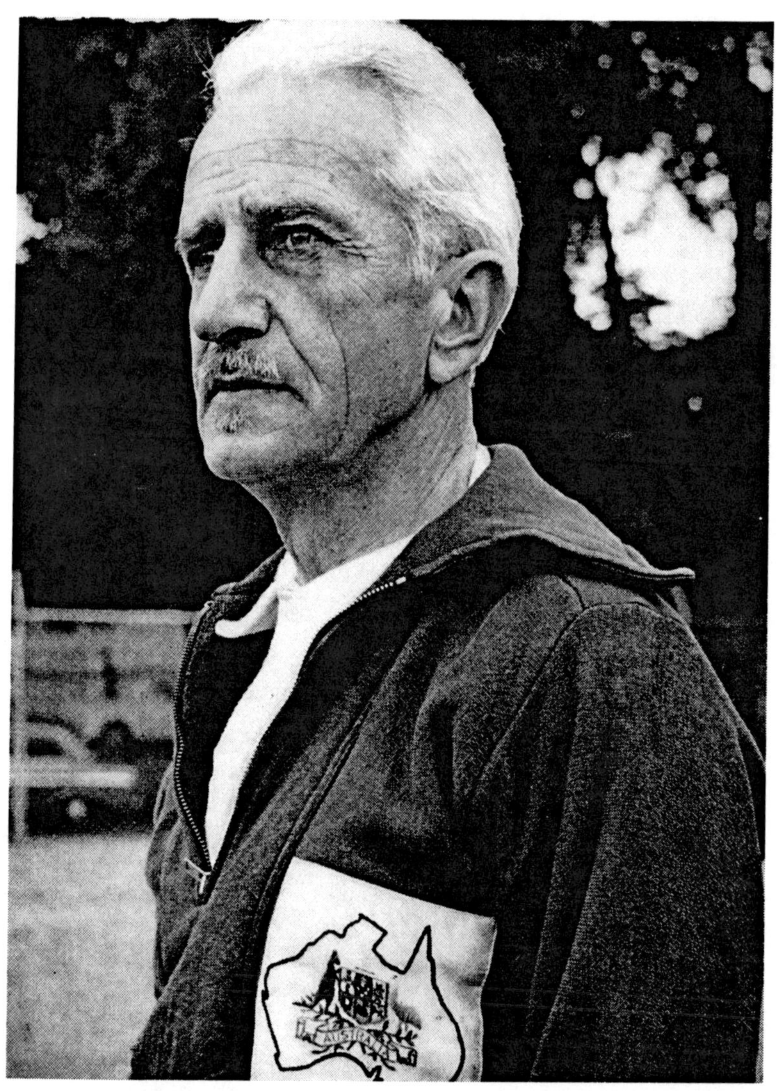

The Author

Official Olympic Coach, Native State Marathon Champion and record-holder at the age of fifty-one years. Holder of the best times run in Australia for fifty miles; sixty miles; and one of three Australians to run more than 100 miles in less than twenty-four hours. This photograph was taken in 1959, when the author was sixty-four.

To paraphrase the statement attributed to Baron Coubertin, the founder of the modern Olympic Games, and to supplement it:

It is not the 'winning' that is important, it is the taking part in.

It is not the 'arrival' that is important, but the journeying to.

It is not the 'doing' that is important, but the trying to be.

All the world admires the 'trier' – and that is something we can all succeed at: be 'tops' in being a sincere and punishing 'trier'.

It is to the 'trier' then, he who would be a champion, that this book is dedicated.

— *Percy Wells Cerutty*

A note about the illustrations

Please note that the photographs have been scanned from the original book, which of course means that the quality of the reproduction has been impacted. We made the decision to include the re-scanned photographs despite the reduced quality for the interest of readers.

Contents

Foreword.................................12

Introduction.............................20

Chapter 1 32

The nature and natural propensities—Gifts and abilities required in the world-class athlete

Chapter 2 56

The necessity of understanding the principles and means of gaining strength and skills

Chapter 3 62

The importance of the naturalistic technique, especially in relation to posture, movement and the physical development of the athlete

Chapter 4 79

The recognition that anything that is inhibited, mechanical, regimented, done under imposed duress or direction, even that which may be thought to be self-imposed – anything at all that is not free outflowing, out-pouring, instinctive and spontaneous, in the end stultifies the objectives, limits the progress, and destroys the possibility of a completely and fully developed personality – athlete and man

Chapter 5 95

An appreciation that 'power rests within us', and great performances in life are produced outside the realm of the fortuitous and the adventitious. That great performance is the result of the intrinsic worth as found and developed in the individual. That great athletes rise and create their destiny

Appendices

Illustrations

(from the original book)

FOREWORD

This book is not intended to be a *complete* text book on athletics, running and field games. Such a vast subject is outside the scope of one volume, as I understand techniques, training and conditioning.

But it *is* intended to be thought–provoking: to stimulate the idea that there may be advanced concepts as yet not found in any text book extant.

It seeks to revive the naturalistic approach to technique as first enunciated by George Hackenschmidt, in his day without peer as an athlete and thinker.

I claim no special gifts, other than, perhaps, some ability to observe, digest, analyse, accept, coupled with an abiding enthusiasm for life and living in all its aspects.

I freely admit my debt to all the great minds that have gone before, from Plato and Aristotle, right through to Newton, Hackenschmidt and Hoffman, the fathers of the modern world athletics era.

I have read widely, on all subjects, ranging from Freud to Krishnamurti, Buddha and Jesus, to Carrell, Jeans and Einstein.

What have these hundred or more 'authorities', scientists, philosophers, to do with world-class athletic performance? I say *everything*, if the athlete would be a *complete* man and not merely a physical exponent of some prowess he may have been gifted with in the first place.

The pure 'physical' instructor, coach or athlete – if such

could be said to exist – could not imagine the realm of 'ideas' that can be applied to high-level athletic performance.

Indeed, the top performances of the future will, increasingly, result from 'spirit' and high intelligence (brains of the first order).

All things will be found to be possible – when we *understand* truly the principles, fundamentals and mysteries.

My thesis is built up on the naturalistic technique.

We have not departed so far from Nature, from the instinctive response, that the child cannot be said to respond naturally and instinctively, in most cases, to his environment.

If we want to get some 'real' clues as to technique, do not study the results or technique 'imagined' by those coaches and teachers who may work things out with their 'brains'.

Thoughts *are* things: and wrong theories, concepts and teachings have ruined more athletes than enough – the process still goes on.

If we turn to a study of the child – his fundamental movements – any runner, if he has the seeing eye, can see *how* to run: even to what point he can train, since children will 'play' until exhausted.

Our athleticism must be, and should be, adult 'play'.

It is when we make it work – dull, routined, scheduled, treadmill work – that we depart from the natural; the joyous; the exhilarating.

Those who subscribe to the printed schedule, the 'daily do-this' coach authority, are little likely to know the joys and pleasures that true athleticism can bring us, young or old.

Perhaps it is because of such wrong concepts and practices, at school and later, that young athletes abandon their athletics instead of making athleticism an integral part of their life pattern.

What these 'authoritative' coaches, these 'do this and that' teachers, these schedule addicts, are responsible for in destroying the natural joys and responses in the young athlete can never be truly known. But it must result in the loss of thousands annually in any country of reasonable size and population.

The athletes who appear to thrive under such teachers, too, would seem to be driven on to their goals by a narrow personal ambition, the determination to 'win' at all or any cost, and know little of the exaltations of the 'free' athlete who trains as he will – in the woods, on the mountains, by the sea.

The emotions are powerful; ambition, jealousy, pride, hate – all these motivate many athletes but they never motivated the greatest athletes.

The truly great ones are motivated by an intense yearning to *express themselves* fully and completely, and athletics is one of the forms in which this expression finds an outlet.

The great athlete is an 'artist' – not merely a 'physical phenomenon'. He may *make* himself into what appears to be a physical phenomenon to others – but he himself knows he is no athletic god – but still a normal, fully functioning man, albeit highly evolved, perhaps, by ordinary standards. A man who is human, even if impervious to the strains and breakdown points of his less evolved brothers, and one who functions emotionally, intellectually, mentally (spiritually) on levels, maybe, the 'ordinary' man may never even guess at. But such an athlete and personality remains, nevertheless, just a man, human and fallible.

This book is to help you to become such a man: a better man: an athlete.

So study the movements of the child up to six or eight years of age.

If you would throw the hammer, the discus, the javelin, enlist the aid of some interested child up to perhaps ten or twelve years. Place a miniature of your apparatus in his hands; indicate what he is to do with it – where to throw it – watch how he *instinctively* goes about doing the job. You may learn much.

The 'brains' of the coach are never to be completely trusted, the observation of many is notoriously faulty. The slow motion camera is a great help, but even then, I have observed, wrong concepts held by coaches cause wrong observation and deductions.

I have been privately horrified, on occasion, when I have observed some technique perfectly executed as in nature (naturalistic technique) and have heard 'authoritative' coaches and athletes condemn some such 'perfect' thing as 'wrong'.

The jumps, high, long and hop step, and the hurdles and pole vault – all these will be outside the scope of the child as to advanced technique, but again his instinctive *approach* – even if not his execution – could be most informative. I commend the idea for serious study.

The technique of athletics requires long, deep and introspective thought by the intelligent athlete. The searching within for the 'feeling' as how to do it.

He must ever learn to depend upon himself, his 'feelings' as to the rightness of things. On the other hand, he must early recognize that many times his feelings, when he attempts anything different or new to him, will tell him that the old, or habitual, is better because it 'feels' more right. It may not be.

Very often we tend to 'feel' the new is wrong because we have been grooved by tradition, the accepted, the orthodox. Heterodoxy always causes emotional and intellectual indigestion. Never reject a new idea, thought, suggestion or conception merely because it is new and we 'feel' it to be wrong.

You will be one of those who stagnate for ever in a childhood state if you do not find that the longer you live, the more unfolds in life and living; that one has to be constantly reassessing, readjusting, rejecting and adopting.

It applies to athletic techniques: much more has to be 'discovered' than ever we have learnt in the past. The unknown can never even be guessed at, it is trite to remark.

You, as an athlete, can march confidently into the future: the 'unknown'. Superior performances will rest, more that ever, in the future developments than in the outmoded techniques, training schedules and ideas of the past. The coach who relies solely upon what has gone before can never build the record-breakers of the future.

The teachings of the coach must always be suspect when he attempts to develop techniques based upon theories worked out intellectually.

Unless he gets the idea from personal experience, and feeling *first*, he is most likely to be wrong in principle.

Such concepts as the rigid schedule, the worked out and laid down day-by-day training routines, find no place in this book, or my ideas as to the fitness of things athletically. Despite the efforts of the industrialist, we are still 'humans' not machines.

Further, the artificial track is *not* the place to develop our athleticism even if it be the place to demonstrate our ability. The track has its place in practising – race practice, I call it – but little or no place in my scheme of things for conditioning and training generally, even for sprinters.

The development of my approach, successful enough in this out-of-the-way corner of the athletic world, athletically backward as it once was, has encouraged me to put my ideas into this book – and before *you*, the discriminating reader, whether coach, athlete or merely curious seeker.

I trust you find something worth while – and to your needs.

PERCY CERUTTY
International Athletic Centre, Portsea, Australia

Coach and pupil on the sandhill at Portsea

The picture shows the nature of the environment: the angle of the hill, the intermittent vegetation and the proximity of the sea.

Note the pinched-on fingers of both runners and the feet sinking into the loose sand. It is this kind of training, carried out consistently for thirty minutes or so, that is beneficial to the athlete, and teaches him to drive with his arms. Without a full driving-arm technique it is very difficult to run the sandhills. Also, the raising of the body-weight by the legs heavily exercises the leg muscles, especially those associated with drive and thrust. The work is natural and pleasant, although most exhausting. When continued to the limits it easily causes vomiting.

Elliott has run our high sandhill some forty-odd times continuously, his last three rungs being the fastest of the series - a kind of sand sprint home. No wonder he excels in last-lap running!

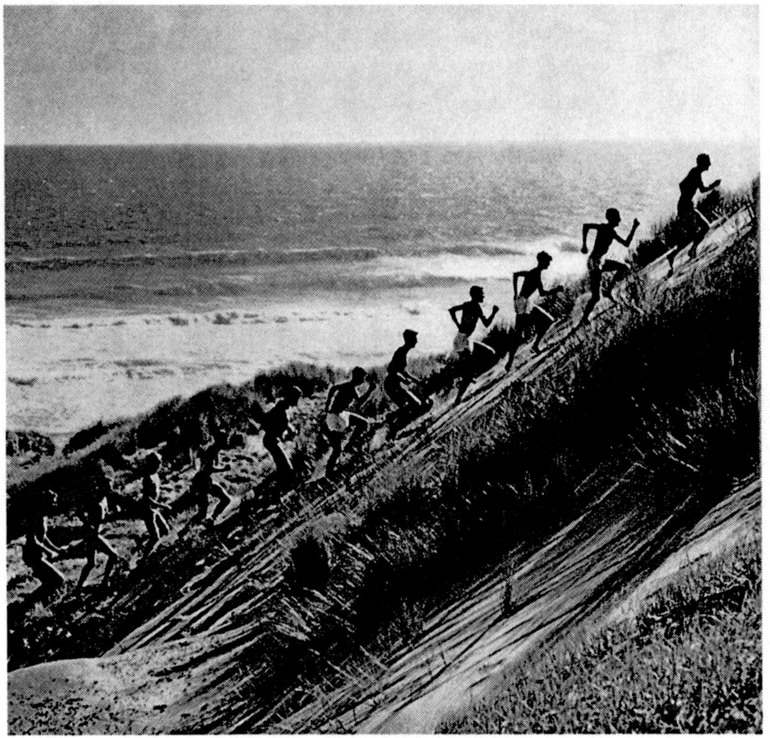

Ten athletes take the sandhill treatment

The coach is merely the leader. Ten athletes is the number of a full 'school', although we can accommodate more if need be. But I find it hard to discover the personality of the athlete if too many are in any one 'school'.

The boys go out for runs in single file through the sand dunes and along the coast, where rough paths exist. They will fun for many miles in this fashion, although in the end the stronger push ahead and the weaker do as best they may. One of the things the boys like doing is to take a new-comer out for such a run for the first time, especially if he is well performed. They have the ability to make even the best very tired, as more than one overseas champion has experienced.

My own ability at this type of training is now reduced to six runs up the sandhill with short recuperative rests between.

The broken waters of the ocean are due to the reefs and rocks under the water on this part of the coast. At low tides these reefs will lift up above the waters, when it is possible to swim among the holes and channels. This is very dangerous and two near-tragedies have occurred, so that deep swimming is forbidden. On the Bay Beach, or at the recognized surf beach, the swimming is safe and controlled. A study of the arm movements of the runners in the picture shows that all are similar, although not exactly at the same part of the stride.

INTRODUCTION

The life at Portsea

How I trained Herb Elliott

ELLIOTT came to me with a best time for the mile of 4:20. He had done little or no serious training in the previous twelve months.

Inspired by his visit to the Melbourne Olympic Games, schoolboy ambitions to be a good runner were revived.

In the beginning he was made to understand that I did not believe in half measures. I did with all my heart and soul what I had to do and I expected my lads to do the same. Nothing less than a 100 per cent full effort, a constant and serious approach, and a determination to get to the top, were good enough for me. Elliott agreed.

We live at Portsea in a beautiful environment, scenically, climatically, athletically.

Incidentally – and I have travelled the world – I know of none better. Within ourselves we are self-contained.

My athletes make their own amusements, which are mostly music, occasional dancing with my daughters and, sometimes, girl friends, and spontaneous acrobatics or acting. We live a full and happy life, no extraneous amusements are sought or seem to be needed.

In Herb's day we only lived at Portsea from Friday evening to Monday morning. Since January 1959 the centre has been conducted 'full time'.

We now live at Portsea. Previously, the rest of the week we lived at South Yarra, close to the centre of the city of Melbourne. Our location was between two extensive park and garden areas ideal for training. The boys could run on park-like terrain for many miles. Variety and change was theirs.

In the beginning Herb was living with an uncle and aunt some miles away, but had access to a large park-like area ideal for his purposes.

He was set to run for thirty minutes to an hour (five to ten miles) before he left for work each morning. This he did a 6 or 6.30 a.m. Each evening, before his evening meal, he trained for about an hour – say ten miles.

Herb applied himself 100 per cent unremittingly. He stepped right into this work, and which is my principle. He could not train Friday evenings, that was taken up travelling to Portsea, although on occasion he has left the car and run the last ten or fifteen miles along the dark country road.

During the week Herb received instruction as to my ideas, philosophy, etc. This is a continuous process that goes on informally, mostly.

Within a year or so most intelligent lads have absorbed all I have to teach. Coincidental with this instruction Herb was taught my technique of movement, the importance of upper body strength, and how to acquire it. He worked assiduously several times a week with the heaviest weights he could move in the exercises I prescribe at Portsea.

He would train two or three sessions each day, never less than one hour, sometimes up to two hours in a session. This work was mostly:

1. Along undulating paths on the cliff tops and ocean beaches.
2. Upon the heavy beach sands.
3. Over the sand dunes, in particular our eighty foot-high sand dune.

4. Along dirt roads, up to twenty miles running.
5. On one of our two beautiful undulating golf links.
6. On the grass of our local playing field.
7. Hall and Stewart circuit running.

Herb applied himself so assiduously, often exhaustingly, that within three months he had improved his mile time to 4:06 whilst still eighteen years of age. Twelve days after his nineteenth birthday he ran 4:00.4 to become Australia one mile champion. At the same meeting he took the Australian 880 yards title in 1:49.3.

A new champion had arrived.

With the cessation of that first track season Herb paid a visit to his home state of Western Australia and had a rest from running of some two or three weeks. He returned to Victoria.

I arranged with Frank Sedgman, of lawn tennis fame, that Herb become a pupil under Stan Nicolles and that he be heavily weight conditioned. Stan Nicolles is a first-class athlete and strong man in his own right – and the inspiration derived from associating with such personalities as Sedgman and Nicolles is very valuable to any youthful and serious athlete. I realize this.

Herb would work seriously and strenuously for a two-hour work-out twice each week. Other work-outs with weights would be done at Portsea or South Yarra where we had ample barbells and other equipment.

On other days Herb would condition heavily with running – doing repetitive runs up the Domain grass slopes, long and continuous runs and varied pace running.

At the weekend, to this type of running would be added Stewart circuit and Hall circuit running, as well as sand, beach and hill work.

A word or two about the Hall and Stewart circuits. The Hall circuit was originated by an athlete who came to me named Gordon Hall, of Geelong. Indeed, it was Hall who introduced John Landy to me and suggested he might have possibilities! Hall had had a holiday in my 'shack' at Portsea and discovered that a rough bush track, one with patches of heavy sand, steep pinches of perhaps forty or fifty feet, and many undulations, existed right at our front gate.

When measured, this roughly rectangular Fartlek course was found to be one mile, one furlong, sixty-three yards. In its earliest days, prior to 1952, the best time recorded on it was 5:57 to Don MacMillan. Alex Henderson, now in the U.S.A. and American two mile record-holder, is another who ran under the six minutes on the Hall circuit.

Since then almost a dozen 'Portsea' athletes have broken the six minutes, the record standing to Herb Elliott with 5:30. To run the Hall circuit in less than six minutes is the ambition of every athlete who comes to Portsea. It is interesting to notice that such redoubtable Australian champions and record-holders as John Landy (he raced over it twice), Les Perry and Geoff Warren all failed in attempts to better the then fabulous six minutes.

The Stewart circuit, discovered and made possible for running by the young English runner, Ian Stewart, is exactly 440 yards in length and starts and finishes outside the property.

It also uses part of the Hall circuit for the first 220 yards, and the runner finishing on it races up the last 110 yards with a grade of one in four or five, on a sandy path. No one to date has bettered one minute dead,[1] Elliott having the best but failing by about half a second to run the even sixty seconds.

Both these circuits are very punishing: The boys run repetitively over them and there is much keenness, timing and interest in the results of their runs.

It will be seen that training at Portsea is strenuous, interesting and produces results. With perhaps not half a dozen exceptions, all the best distance and middle distance runners in Australia have been conditioned on these circuits, the Hall circuit in particular since it was evolved some years ago.

This form of training brings with it a lot of enthusiastic competition between the boys. Nothing is ever done half-heartedly; the tradition is tremendous and carried on by the boys (athletes) themselves. Each athlete chooses, mostly, the terrain he wishes to use.

It is not unusual for an athlete to visit the grassed oval (where I give instruction each weekend) and after our teaching session ask to be excused as he wishes to run on the sandhill or the beach. I favour that 'free expression' and encourage the lads to be self-determining, my role being mostly a supervising and advising one.

I attribute the attitudes of my athletes, their initiative, confidence and willingness to believe they can run a world record, to this approach. To me, each must learn to decide for himself; and as quickly as possible. That it has 'paid off' would appear to be certain.

My athletes are in no way appalled by world records, and it is justified, I feel, to mention that eight world records have been set by athletes who have trained at Portsea on these various terrains, whilst all Australian records from the 880 yards to the six miles have been set and reset for many years by Portsea-trained, sand-, hill-, track- and golf link-conditioned athletes.

This type of training was employed by Herb continuously through our winter months, an overall period of six months. As we approach our track season, around September – October, which is our spring, we intensify our work and tend to do more fast running on the golf links and less extensive work on the sand and the two circuits, Hall and Stewart.

Not that that type of work ever ceases but the intensity of the work is definitely accelerated. Herb, as all others, is then expected to train so that he conditions the organism to running at full predetermined racing speeds, and, also, holding a hard effort for the duration of the race, or event, aimed at.

It seems to me that 'interval' type of training ignores the fact that if the organism grows accustomed to ceasing an effort, resting and then resuming the effort, to a pseudo-scientific formula, the athlete will tend to respond to this conditioned reflex, and it would appear that the failure of this form of training, which appears to be general (when viewed from the standards I set), could be due to ignoring this factor.

What is true, as far as Australia is concerned, is that athletes, coaches and officials all over the Continent have found that no champion has been 'produced' strictly in conformity with interval-type training, and I have had the same statements made to me by disillusioned athletes and coaches in the U.S.A., England and Europe.

However this may be, Elliott has never been conditioned to interval training, and we never use a stopwatch in our work except to check the resultant speeds derived from the use of various techniques. The watch is used for *evidence* only, never as a set or arbitrary standard for effort.

I hold that the human being cannot be reduced to the status of a machine – and I attribute the success of the athletes who received their early training at Portsea on my specialized Fartlek methods, not so much to the initial ability of the athletes, but to the form of training we favour at Portsea, and the terrain we train upon. The introduction of resistance in the form of sand and hill is too important to be ignored and the track can never fulfil the lack nor the scientific formula replace 'natural and instinctive' effort.

However that may be, this much is true – no Australian has set a world record who was not conditioned at some time at Portsea or was developed, mainly, on the lines applied to Elliott. A further word may not go amiss about the use of stopwatches in training.

Firstly let us consider that there are two schools of thought in the world. The first believes the brain can 'think' up all that is needed. That the brain is 'all' – has superseded Nature, even God.

If this is not acceptable to you as true, consider how Christians have devised prayers and petitions, if not telling God what they want, what He should do, at least urging with strong petitions, flatteries and grovellings, what they – these 'brains' – *think* should be done!

So it is with 'academic' coaches. They assume the psyche is nothing; that the unconscious mind (instinct) can no longer be trusted; that we cannot measure off time or effort accurately; that everything must be subjected to 'science', the prescribed, the schedule, the stopwatch.

Then there is the other school, the mystical natures, perhaps, who sense how it should be done; who learn how they can trust themselves, Nature; who, instead of instructing God, as it were, are instructed *by* God – or Nature.

These coaches seek – and seeking, find. It is to this category I belong. I early learnt that Nature is in us and can measure out time to a fraction of a second, when we learn to trust her without equivocation, absolutely and finally. It is true it is good to make checks – that is, I will observe Elliott running and check his speed for my edification over, say, 200 metres, but he never uses a watch, and is not always informed as to the time, and has learnt to trust himself.

Therefore he has no inhibitions as to speed or records, but runs as he can and should, that is, like Nurmi, merely to win with certainty, as he does. Just how fast he could run the mile neither he nor anyone else can even guess, but this is certain – it is far below his world record of 3:54.5, just as Nurmi and Zatopek, reproduced in a later age, would have run faster and been just as far in front!

However this is just too much for most of those who trust their brain, have surrendered their instincts, and, like the politician, believe all can be achieved through 'brain power' – wisdom, intelligence and 'spirit' being factors associated with dreamers and idealists: which is true, although it is customary to imagine that dreamers and idealists are incapable of being 'realists' and active.

Actually, it is the 'dreamers and idealists' who lead the world to higher ends and who – when they are active, as most are –

are the only true 'realists'. It is interesting that, whilst I know I am often dismissed as a dreamer and idealist, I often feel I am one of the most 'realist' of people I know. Those who contest me soon find that out!

When an athlete comes to Portsea he has to forget most or all he has been taught by others. If he has never had a coach he is fortunate, and my task is easier. I teach an original technique based on my own researches as to primitive man, animals, and, above all, our own Australian aboriginals – the people indigenous to Australia.

This race, cut off from all other cultures and civilizations for countless thousands of years, is, as far as I have discovered, the *only* race of people from whom we can learn how God or Nature truly expected us to move over the ground. In a word, they appear to me to be, until contaminated by civilization, the only perfect movers – posture, walking and running – in our world. *And they move differently to all other peoples.* Put their feet to the ground *differently*. Hold themselves *differently*. Carry their arms *differently*.

This is what I teach. (It is true there are odd people in all races who move similarly. Arthur Newton was one. I can think of others.) Therefore the embryo champion spends much time, at first, mastering the art, not easy for some, of putting their feet correctly to the ground, holding their body *up* by the use of their abdominals and back muscles, and developing, varying and driving through the various speeds by the deliberate and conscious use of their arms, until this technique becomes normal, natural and unconscious.

In the beginning Elliott was subjected to just these teachings and was expected to run behind me to learn how it is done, in actual practice, i.e. by running.

Elliott proved apt. He did not need to be told anything twice. His progress, like his subsequent performances, was phenomenal. He achieved in days what it often took others months. (Some never learn, or cannot be taught, rather!) Hence his rapid progress.

After all it is more *mind* (personality and inherent gifts) than brain – that modern deceptive product of this materialistic age. When I speak of mind I mean mind-spirit: that 'awareness' I view as a separate state or condition to 'brain' which too often is brain-cunning. Indeed I make a definite distinction here.

Hence, and incidentally, I am not of the school of thought that relies on tactics, cunning, letting the other fellow do the work then jump him in the final burst, and so on – that success is despised by the better type of mind and personalities. I do not believe that winning at any and all costs is better than running well; rather acquit oneself as a 'man' than win by some of the dubious tactics I see.

All these concepts were taught to Herb, and, I have no doubt at all, contributed markedly to his success, since he had the nature to be able to absorb them whole-heartedly and without reservations. Very quickly such teachings, made real and factual, are part of athletes such as Elliott, and it is not difficult to understand how they may even consider they 'were always that way' – that is, in short, they *knew*, before they were taught!

What is true is that theirs is the mind and temperament that easily responds to the higher teachings, both of life and athletics.

It is my practice, at least once in the weekend, to have a teaching session on the oval. There I can, with the athletes, discuss and demonstrate every aspect of technique, training and racing. I can but repeat, Elliott proved an apt pupil and fulfilled my full anticipations as to attitudes and performances. I had expected him to run 3:55 for the mile and he did just that with half a second to spare.

And so the work went on. Steadily, methodically, surely and with reasonable certainty as to anticipated results. And no day seemed too long, and no weather too discouraging.

At Portsea the boys are mostly abroad around 6.30 to 7 a.m.

ertain amount of active movement, to and from, ›nversation: then silence. They have gone. They will ast an hour, down on the beaches, through the bush roaus, ...g the cliff tops. Then they bathe in the ocean breakers – as naked as innocence itself – shouting and tumbling in the waves. Then it is over and a hungry bunch of inspired athletes return noisily for breakfast, which is already prepared.

With what avidity do these hungry ones seize their bowls: help themselves to their rolled oats, dried fruits, raisins, walnuts and bananas. These bowls are of considerable size and the food, all eaten raw and dry (no milk or any fluid at all is added), takes some twenty minutes to eat and masticate properly.

Then come lightly poached eggs, potatoes chipped (french fried) in oil, followed by good brown wholemeal bread (not always easily obtainable, unfortunately) with marmalade, honey, Vegemite, treacle – almost anything of that nature.

No fluid is taken with this meal, neither water, tea, milk or coffee. The athletes are expected to have taken ample fluid (water) before coming to the table.

The next athletic session is usually around twelve o'clock (noon) but can commence as early as 11 a.m., or as late as 1 p.m.

If it is a session at the grassed oval it is punctually at noon and ceases about 1.30 p.m. If very hot, it will cease at 1 p.m. when we all travel the half mile to the pier (or bay) beach, there to swim and dive and enjoy the amenities of this famous, but exclusive, resort.

I say exclusive, since nothing could be as unlike as Portsea is to famous resorts such as Nice. There is no city or town. It is a village in which most of the houses are rather costly, and many are quite grand affairs, with tennis courts and extensive gardens.

The actual beach and scenery at the pier, in my opinion, equals anything I have seen abroad. However, it is not magnificent, no mountains, but beautiful with its shrub-covered cliffs, deep blue waters, golden sands. The whole beach is no longer than three-quarters of a mile. Boats, launches, yachts, canoes abound. Everything is clean and gay. Surely a favoured place.

After an hour or so the boys return for lunch. Fruit and vegetable salads, mild cheeses, herrings in tomato sauce, hard-boiled eggs, wholemeal bread and one pint of fresh milk each. The salad dressing is of olive oil and lemon juice.

Then follows the siesta: an inviolable rule: all go to bed, mostly to sleep soundly for about two hours. Around 5 p.m. all are awake again, refreshed and full of vigour for the final session of the day. According to the season, the weather and one's own inclination, so it is the sand, hill or beach, the oval or the golf links. The golf links are mostly favoured.

The boys will run on them very hard, varying pace with the undulations. They are taught to learn to run fast by using the downgrades, and to fight as in a finishing sprint by tearing into the upgrades – all without any spells – my runners never do more than ease up – actually walking or stopping is looked upon as 'weakly' and I am the only one forced to resort to it. My lungs just will not take the continuous effort, although I am able to maintain quite reasonable speeds in the early stages of the training.

The efforts often put out in these sessions have to be seen to be believed, experienced to realize what we call 'training' at Portsea. It is not uncommon for the boys to return home exhausted, sweat pouring from their all but naked brown bodies. With the exhaustion is an exhilaration – due to environment – the 'power' and the fellowship.

The lovely views, the well-kept grassed terrain of the golf links, amongst the best of our seaside courses, the invariably beautiful sunsets – all play their part in the development of the athlete, and Herb revelled in it all.

So the last session is over, darkness is falling, the boys are back; in the colder months to gather around the alcove stove, in the warmer to rest on the bunks and divans, with music from calypso to Italian opera, from Josephine Baker to Bach and

Beethoven, is the order of the day until bedtime.

The evening meal is always an animated affair. Much play is made of the success or otherwise of the training efforts, the runs on the circuits, Hall and Stewart, the miles on the oval, the experiences on golf links or sand dune. The food is mostly vegetables, conservatively cooked, the fluid extract resulting from the cooking of the vegetables being greatly esteemed as an elixir, which it is.

Large plates are piled high, since we enjoy, possibly, as large and beautiful vegetables as are to be found in the world. Cauliflowers twice as large as a man's head, cabbages four to six times as large, carrots and parsnips – a meal, almost, in one! Peas, beans, sprouts – every conceivable vegetable and plenty, really plenty, of potatoes chipped, in oil or baked in their jackets in the oven.

Animal fats are never used in our cooking. Fish and poultry prevail, or minced steak cooked as hamburgers with onion. The boys never tire of our simple but health and strength-providing foods, their appetites whetted by the sauce of wind, spray, sea, sky, track, sand and healthy appetite creating exercise.

Seldom is less than twenty miles covered in the day's training, yet it seems 'fun', is fun, and is as happy and as pleasurable a way to live, apart from the athletic ends, as surely any 'healthy' young man could wish for, or enjoy.

Half a pint of milk is taken with this meal, only. The dessert is invariably fruit salad with the 'top of the milk' whipped into a frothy cream; no extra cream is ever bought and thus the balance of cream (fat) protein and carbohydrates in the milk is reasonably maintained even if not consumed together.

There is no stint of this food. The appetite of each is governed by simple hunger, and soon the very tired ones are dozing over books, then to bed, until it is usual, by 10.30 p.m., for the whole 'camp' to be asleep—and so ends another day at Portsea.

1. *Since writing the above, the record has been lowered to 58.5 by Alan Broadbent, a Victorian 220– and 440–yards runner. – Percy Cerutty, 1964*

Chapter 1

The nature and natural propensities – Gifts and abilities required in the world-class athlete

A discursive discussion

I take my stand on the statement that the great athlete is born to his greatness. But this cannot be taken to mean that in the beginning he, the athlete, realizes this, or that early in life he necessarily shows marked evidence of his later greatness.

But I do say that when such an athlete looks back to his childhood he will realize that he *did* have certain gifts, even if they did not appear particularly to distinguish him at that time; that he did feel certain convictions as to himself or his *right* and ability to excel in something.

As he progresses through his early years, life and its affairs will seem to conspire towards certain ends and he may realize he is being 'borne along' or feel an 'end-point' – of being a 'victim of his destiny'.

I can recall to mind many great athletes who grew up and lived that way.

Gundar Haegg, as a boy, became interested in running, in the mountains where he was reared. I have visited the area, which is many miles from the rail head – there is no town or village. Yet Haegg must have learnt of the great runners – or perhaps of just some athlete who was his hero.

What is true is that he did run as a boy, and later, as a youth, went up to the city environment where his talents and ambitions were enabled to attain fulfilment.

The tragedy of Haegg's athletic career, as with his co-competitor Arne Andersson's, was his exclusion as an amateur, another illustration of the narrowness of the application of the amateur code.

Clubs, promoters, newspaper journalists, officials, even countries, can gain kudos and prestige, but when the athlete who helps produce all this accepts his share in augmented expenses he is deemed a professional and excluded. How utterly puerile and dishonest.

So these two great athletes were lost to the sport they adorned: a result truly criminal to one as ardent as I am.

It is to the credit of the country of Finland that although the great Nurmi was also forced out of world amateur competition and the Olympic Games, by international action, his country, although it had officially to implement his exclusion, never appeared, in actual fact, to have excluded him as an amateur in Finland, his home country.

It is not recorded whether he ever competed again as an amateur or not – but he appears to have enjoyed the confidence of his amateur countrymen, to have remained an honoured name and official throughout his lifetime, and when the Olympic Games were held in his capital city of Helsinki in 1952, it was Nurmi, no other, the 'excluded and rejected amateur', who first traversed the track sacred to the dedication of amateurism.

Nurmi carried the torch round the arena and lit the symbolic flame. What irony, what cause for winces which seemed, at the time, to pass completely unfelt. Such is the hardened and impenetrable skin of official amateurism, one of the 'wonders of the modern athletic age – and one of the greatest hypocrisies mankind accepts and babbles oath and affirmations about – 'in man's many babblings'.

The destined great athlete will look back and in retrospect

will recognize the inevitability of his whole life, the extraordinary 'chance' happenings, maybe, but recognizing the 'pattern' of it all. He will realize his destiny was in this way: that in some vague and indefinable manner he always knew it – and that the ultimate accomplishments were also as inevitable and certain.

This feeling, this recognition, this inevitability, is felt of observed in the lives of all those destined to make their mark somewhere, sometime and in something, whatever it may be, and is not necessarily confined to athletics.

Great people and great athletes realize early in their lives their destiny, and accept it. Even if they do not consciously realize the how, the where, the what.

It is this feeling of inevitability (predestination) that can be accepted and acted upon. When it is strong it will persist through life – and it will be in exact relation to the results seen and achieved.

Therefore, it is an infinite variable, much stronger in some than in others and totally absent, or almost non-existent, in the many. Not having it, they do not miss it.

It is not given to all coaches or teachers to detect and fully recognize the gifted. Far from it, in fact. Anyone at all can recognize the prodigy. His early evidence of outstanding ability makes it self evident. But it requires more than ordinary perspicacity to detect the inherent power and ability latent in the 'late gifted' – those whose achievements tend to come late in life, as indeed did Newton's, a classical example, if ever we needed one, to illustrate this point.

Newton's athletic career commenced only at thirty-nine years of age. Earlier in his life he had done some running, apparently without conspicuous success. He had abandoned all such activities and embarked upon the prosaic career of a farmer in South Africa, where he had emigrated from his native England.

As a farmer he had rapidly achieved marked success and

won prizes for his cotton and tobacco – but he failed in a singular manner to foresee causes that eventually forced him off his farmlands.

It was as a protest, says Newton, that he took up running. To me – and I came to know the man well – his running was as much an inevitable part of his destiny, and the man himself, as breathing. At least this is my opinion, formed many years ago, and I am not budging from it, despite any Newtonian assertions to the contrary.

The man was, and is still, a phenomenon. He was born to run, and to do other things as well, *superlatively*, and he did them.

Schweitzer in Africa is just such another, operating in another field. I could cite many, in all walks of life.

Any fool, even, can recognize the gifts and the abilities of the 'early gifted', and predict 'great careers'. So, also, the prodigy, who soars up like a rocket in a blaze of glory, often before his 'late gifted' brother is out of athletic knickerbockers, as it were.

But as quickly does his brilliance depart into the dark limbo of the forgotten. By twenty years of age, often his athletic powers have left him, he is a spent force – a name and a disappointment.

The career of the 'early gifted' can often be long, successful, complete and satisfactory. It is he who can run a world record-time, perhaps, before the late-gifted have even started in on their equally satisfactory, efficient and successful careers.

In the category of the early gifted we have athletes such as Pirie, D. Johnson, W. G. George, to name three Englishmen that occur to me, and in the second category of the late gifted we have the Zatopeks and Kutses, with Newton as an extreme example as mentioned above.

Athletics and, indeed, all sports teem with examples of big, powerful, early developed and matured types, who, as boys and youths, are able to perform equally with, and even outdo, fully grown and matured athletes.

These lads and schoolboys are often of the prodigy type, as already mentioned. One of the foolishnesses of the age is putting all schoolboys and youths into 'age' categories and extolling the performances of these early developed, and often overgrown, types as fully meritorious.

That this is so can easily be one of the major reasons for the fact that so many of these big and promising, early gifted and prodigy types fail to go on to maintain in maturity the gifts and performances of their youth.

It well may be that their comparatively easily attained successes, being 'whales amongst minnows', deprive them of the recognition of the need for struggle: in a word, their intrinsic worth is undermined: they never learn what it is to have to sweat and suffer sufficiently. They get big results on little training effort and suffer few setbacks or disappointments.

As life is, as they go up the scale of the years, they find that year by year they are increasingly overtaken by those who once seemed so far behind in gifts, ability and performances.

Where once the schoolboy championship was a 'push-over', now the senior one is highly competitive and success far from certain.

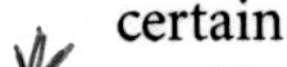

These 'early successful' types, little toughened by the setbacks and struggles that develop the qualities for success in others, wilt and give up.

By twenty-four years of age they have retired: 'too old', they say, with an apologetic grin, that too often betokens the disappointment – and lack of comprehension as to 'why' – that is theirs.[1]

In actual fact, physical maturity, as far as certain aspects of our physiology is concerned, is only arrived at gradually. For a career to be finished when in truth it should only be arriving at the stage of full development is both a tragedy in the case of the individual and a loss to a country, when athletic prowess in the Olympic Games counts for so much, nationally. It will count even more in future years.

It is no wonder then that 'late-gifted' types, such as Zatopek and Kuts, find, after twenty-five years of age, that they have the field almost to themselves! Their early gifted companions are then hardly in evidence, much less the prodigies. Chataway's name suggests itself in the first category, and the two Seamans, one in U.S.A. and the other in England, in the latter category, if you need illustrations.

I do not name these athletes to be gratuitously offensive in any way, but merely as illustrations. What they can do about it, in the case of the Seamans, I do not know. We have similar types in Australia. Australian record class, even world record-breakers at seventeen and eighteen years, where are they at twenty, much less twenty-four, years!

Australian sport – and especially swimming and tennis – teems with examples. Record-breakers at as early as fourteen and fifteen years as swimmers, but still children really; finished, Out of the game, retired, before attaining to voting-age, full citizenship, adulthood.

To me it is crazy and reflects adversely as to Australian national conceptions. Or is it typical of our immaturity as a nation and a people? – which may be merely a precocity without real maturity and substance. It may easily be so.[2]

On the other hand it may as easily be – even more so than in the case of the U.S.A., the home of the athletic prodigy who doesn't go on – evidence of things and performances to come. Something to come when the national consciousness is awakened to the talent we have, and the worth-whileness from a national health, fitness and prestige point of view, is appreciated, which it is not as I write.

On the contrary, athletics, still looked upon as possessing a freakish and juvenile quality only to be valued every four years – at Olympic Games time – is put a bad last in the national scheme and evaluation of things. Success in business – even if the successful one dies before fifty! – success in politics, success in almost anything is valued before success in the real business of living, living healthily, actively, artistically.

We were fortunate that John Landy, although he showed gifts as a schoolboy, did not display outstanding ability or the precocity of the child athletic prodigy.

Landy merely kept narrowly ahead of his schoolboy contemporaries, and set no juvenile records that I ever heard of. In his late teens he was beaten by others, and what Landy attained to he earned every yard of a long and persistently travelled way.

Landy's real monument is himself, not his mile record. More than most athletes, he set out to make himself into something, and although he may have been disappointed in not achieving some of the 'details' of his career, he did achieve the primary and vital one – an undisputed, clear-cut record.

In the beginning I enthused Landy as to his goals and possibilities, encouraged him, and in my exhortations and personal achievements, if I may say so, showed him the 'way'.

That Landy mostly travelled it alone is both a tribute to his personality and his greatness, as it is the reason that he did not rise to greater heights as a competitive athlete.

By nature John Landy was not competitive in the sense that Zatopek was competitive, or Bannister, or Elliott. An idealist, a man with a mission – to prove himself to himself – Landy achieved his ends and aims. His end and aim was not beating this one or that – but in achieving, if only once, a superlative performance.

Landy did just that, and proved by his consistent miling that his record was no fluke or freakish performance.

That Landy and his gifts in the beginning were so little recognized, both publicly and officially, is evidenced by the fact that he was placed last on the list of athletes chosen to represent Australia in the Olympic Games in 1952.

Also, Landy was one of those who had to find his own funds to represent his country, as did many another in that same team and year. Had these funds not been forthcoming from private sources, it is not inconceivable that John Landy, his name and career, would never have been heard of in the realm of athletics.

Both Landy and I knew he should have been placed higher, and John felt so badly about it that he decided not to go to Helsinki. That I persuaded him is now history, but significant.

He knew, and I recognized, his *potential.* The selectors of the team can hardly be blamed for not realizing this.

Almost immediately on arrival in England, before going to Helsinki for the Games, he set an all-comers British two mile record of 8:54.

In few countries would amateur sport be so little supported financially by the government of the country. The hit-and-miss attitudes even to participation in the Olympic Games is a byword and Australia succeeds as well as she does in spite of – not because of – any national or governmental support or interest. There isn't any! The Melbourne Olympic Games notwithstanding. *That* was a freakish happening, resulting from a small group of enthusiasts. As I write, there are not six cinder tracks in the length and breadth of the whole country.

'Dave' Stephens was an even more interesting case of the late-gifted. It took ten years, from fifteen years of age to twenty-five years, for Stephens to indicate that he was anything but 'another club runner of promise', but little else. He was twenty-five years of age before he was considered good enough to represent his State of Victoria in an Australian championship!

However, this runner persisted, never entirely gave up hope of 'getting somewhere', as he would put it. He never questioned where or how. I despaired for him often. Failure after failure.

His case looked hopeless. But Stephens went on to run a world record that at the time of its accomplishment was outstanding, even more so than John Landy's record in the mile, relatively. Stephens ran 27:54 for six miles and was the only man, other than Zatopek, to break twenty-eight minutes. He beat Zatopek's best records, a feat far more difficult than beating Haegg's mile record, as did Bannister and so many more since. To this day only two men have ever run six miles faster than Stephens.

Without any special gifts, physically or mentally, to sustain him, David Stephens, of Australia, stands as an example of what persistence – never giving up entirely – can do. Without great strength, he mastered the art of running *over* the ground with the minimum of physical effort as never before or since. His efficiency, yet economy of effort, had to be seen to be believed.[3]

Dave Stephens failed in the Games in Melbourne. The cards had been stacked against him, with injuries and upsets. He can never be written off as a failure. On the contrary, Stephens must shine as the one prime example, if any be needed, of where an ordinary, normal in every way, young man may get if he never entirely gives up – believes in himself and maybe, of course, finds someone to support him in his 'impossible'(?) tasks and crazy (so-called) efforts.

His 'beginnings' – as were Landy's – were at Portsea: his 'way' the barbell and the sandhill way: his sacrifices were to abandon himself *completely* for a time to accomplish his objectives.

What Stephens and Landy have done, hundreds, I could almost say, could do better. This is true as to ability. It may not be true as to intrinsic worth: character. That has to be developed, earned. The growth of both was nurtured in the peace of the ti-tree and the sandhills of Portsea, Victoria, and where I write of their deeds, as now.

If these results can be achieved in a country as remote and backward, athletically, as Australia – where less than ten years previously the national mile record had stood officially at 4:14, and where to run six miles in thirty-two minutes was considered an outstanding achievement, and where to do better than either, in professional running in this country, can still be considered an achievement! – so much for amateurism, where it outdoes the so-called professional and in many ways outdoes him, the professional, in the kudos, prestige, trips and perquisites generally! Surely it is a topsy-turvy world, at least athletically, as we find it in Australia. Tennis amateurs 'live' on their sport, mostly the year round, whilst professional runners, excluded from Olympic Games participation, go to workaday jobs and compete on Saturdays and holidays and are excluded from receiving lucrative scholarships to the U.S.A.

So the coach must take them as they come, and the athlete learn to keep on keeping on, as a paint advertisement has it, since no one knows to what heights he may achieve – and aspiring is no crime, yet!

In other respects they come in all guises – the quiet ones, the noisy ones, the ardent and enthusiastic ones. Like Zatopek, who carved out his own route and methods. And those who, like Chataway, have to be prodded into it, if we are to believe what we read!

In this regard it is easy to see that the enthusiast – the pioneer – carries more guns and will get further ahead of another who, in the beginning, may have much greater gifts, if that other lacks certain qualities, as he may.

After all, nothing really worth while has ever been accomplished *without* enthusiasm, although some men appear to get to relatively great heights without an overdose of the commodity in their natures. However, in their quiet, dour and persistent way even the less demonstrative and ebullient will be enthusiastic enough, and will show it by fighting, when threatened, and if they *do* achieve worth-while goals.

What do we look for, then? How can the great athlete-to-be recognize himself. He cannot.

The coach, even the best and most experienced, must reserve judgment. Too many swans-to-be prove only to be ducks, while many an ugly duckling, in the beginning, can mature into a great athlete.

In any world-class field, say for a mile or a marathon, could we pick the champion on appearances. Many who excel do not seem to have one great contributing feature – on the surface!

Too much rests in the personality of the tyro and embryo champion. I never try to pick them – they pick themselves, as I state elsewhere.

Of course, I will have ideas, even strong opinions, but I am rarely conclusive, for has it not been said that the stone rejected by the builders may often become the keystone of the arch? •

Athletes, it is good to be a rejected one – occasionally! Nothing conspires more than rejection to bring out your qualities of greatness – if you have any! It is by these things we know them – and you can begin to know yourself.

Be on your guard against early success – that underminer of the building of the future, that quicksand upon which many a big career has foundered and been swept away.

If you are gifted and have easily won early success, grow to hate 'rewards', praise, flatteries – and those who bestow them. All this is heterodox I know.

If you are truly great you will realize the truth of what I say as you read it. If you reject my words – you will be 'less-great' by just that much.

To be a great runner it is not essential to be born an 'Adonis' or perfect man–competition winner. It is not even essential that you attain average height – you can weigh from six to sixteen stone and still succeed in some event, although I would fancy you for the marathon more than the mile if you weighed only eighty-four pounds, and for the hammer or the shot put rather than either running event, if your weight is in the order of 224 lb.!

But there *is* an event for *everyone*. That is the great feature about athletics. This cannot be said of world-class football, for example.

But it is essential to be strong, or to make oneself strong – *very* strong – today.

Would you sprint? Then lack of inches need not stop you

if you have all the other requisites – Eddie Tolan of the past and Ira Murchison of the present, as well as Agostini, are evidence of short men performing great deeds – if any such evidence or examples be needed.

Don MacMillan, Australia's first great miler, if we omit Gerald Backhouse – was six feet three inches tall and weighed in like a weight-lifter or wrestler. At one time, in Australia's national mile championship, the diminutive Leslie Perry, five feet five inches and weighing only some 126 lb. or so, was the regular runner-up to Macmillan.

I never heard anyone refer to the incongruity of size in the spectacle. Great 'small' men always appear bigger on the track than their actual size and weight. And big ones – well, they look what we seem to expect, when champions.

After all, mostly everyone sees personality and performance – first.

Ignore, then, whether you are tall and thin or short and stocky – whether they laughed at you at home (where they are often unkind) or at school (where they *are* mostly blind, anyway).

Indeed – to hell with the lot of them if you 'feel' you can do it.

But on the whole, good big ones tend to beat good little ones. You can be the exception to prove the rule of course.

But take nothing for granted: especially appraise carefully the person, coach, teacher, friend or parent making an appraisement of you, whether favourable or unfavourable. They may or may not be right.

It is important that you do not make a mistake as to *their* judgment, rather than accept what that judgment may be.

Remember few in the world are *trained*, disciplined, or have suffered enough to be *absolutely* honest and sincere, even if reasonably knowledgeable.

Then, being a parent or even a school teacher does not presuppose one has a ha'p'orth of genuine knowledge, or wisdom, even common sense. Both occur in millions – the two former, I mean; the latter three are still rather rare, unique.

Indeed, the greatest single disillusionment the child suffers is to learn that one parent is not a god nor the other an angel; and for athletes that coaches rarely bother to think deeply and give, often, the most cursory, casual and off-hand answers and opinions.

Later comes the realization that they do not really know – have been mostly bluffing throughout their careers! At least one fully qualified State coach admitted this to me (as to the 'knowing' and bluffing)! He was honest and had 'parts' and did quite good work: the others – who knew it and didn't admit it, or, worse, didn't know it, if that is possible – well, they continued busily to ruin quite good prospects.

I believe in the open mind, the mind open to possibilities, the mind with a definite bias to giving every athlete the benefit of the doubt – a chance, even many chances, to prove his possible worth.

Prove him a failure *after* his career is finished; whilst there is life there can be some hope of singular success – for all. It may be after a career that leaves one short of championships that one turns to the marathon, as did Stanley and Prentice in Australia, and Peters in England. The first two to become national champions and record-holders, Peters to become the fastest man in the world at this event in his day:

It is wrong to assume that we can accurately determine any athlete's propensities at an early age.

So the coach must learn to take them as they come. I have in mind the coach who is interested to build champions. The case of the coach who teaches in a school or similar institution is different. He performs mostly a mundane task and is paid to perform it. Personally, I have never been interested along such lines of endeavour, and my message, if any, is for the specialized coach of the ambitious athlete.

Not that anyone can be indubitably dubbed one or the other exclusively. In athletics one is all and all can try to be that one!

The coach can often see the promise in a lad, but only too often inherent defects in personality, which only become apparent with maturity, mar and blight the promise.

Too many, apparently gifted, fail to fulfil in any spectacular way their early promise, and the grandiose scheme of Cecil Rhodes, which attempts to pre-determine by appraisement of early all-round qualities, has lamentably failed, in my opinion, to justify the optimism and huge expenditure of both Rhodes and his ideas. It is not so easy.

The scholarship scheme that bears Rhodes's name attempted to pre-determine the type, and to choose them, who could be trained as leaders in society: Empire builders, what-have-you.

In view of the amplitude of the scheme, few are thrown up who even, it seems to me, make more than an average mark in later life.

So it can be with the athlete and athletics.

Especially is this so of university types. Those favoured young men of whom it is confidently predicted that they will become the national leaders: they seldom do. I ignore the U.S.A. tradition where it is customary to offer scholarships in abundance to otherwise non-academic types merely because of their sporting prowess.

I have in mind those of mental qualities, apparently, above average, physically above average, what we would term 'of good standing'.

In Australia the universities, which once produced sequences of first-class athletes, singularly fail to do so any longer. There could be many reasons, at least, in Australia – although Oxford and Cambridge, in England, continue to produce their quotas of distinguished athletes.

But approach the matter as we may, the real champion will

be found to have a good brain and it is far from being disadvantageous that it is not conditioned in the university schools of any country.

With the good brain will be an enquiring mind, usually a lively personality and a marked suspicion of the orthodox and traditional.

I count it a defect if the athlete is not normally repelled and antagonistic to any rigid schedule which prescribes sequences of fast and slow training efforts, usually in the order of the 440 yards or 400 metres.

Such mechanical, stereotyped and regimented forms of track training, surely such methods – unimaginative and lacking all joy – can have no common denominator with the concepts of amateur athleticism and the freeing of the whole personality.

Rather must they make for the conditioned response, the treadmill means to a dubious objective as far as the personality of the athlete is concerned. I will have nothing of it.

And this is true whether a coach sets the formalized schedule or the athlete conspires to set his own. The damage to the personality in his formative years will be the same.

There must be no set schedule, no daily direction that is fixed and pre-calculated. Nothing at all, I would say, that rigidly based in authority, whether imposed from without or within. And all this despite the results of both Zatopek and Landy, both rather dedicated, it would appear, to the formalized style of training. Both, however, enjoyed and advocated much Fartlek running in the woods and the like.

Indeed, in the case of Landy, in his later years much of his training was done running in the foothills of the Australian Alps. He had proper track at all to train upon, except in those rare weeks when he returned to his home in Melbourne.

I know of no truly great athlete or personality who has appeared as a result of this modern trend to formalized, repetitive, scheduled track training. Nor do I foresee any.

On the contrary I expect to see many who otherwise may have been greater, bogged down in this popular nostrum of the day. In the beginning it may have had certain justifications, but in the hands or minds of those incompetent to know, it has seized upon the meretricious and imposed it upon the young and credulous.

Already the substance of this form of training has been found missing, and increasingly in this country, Australia, at least, have the athletes of promise turned away from the interval form of repetitive effort.

Those without the ability to think deeply, or feel acutely, will always tread the treadmill of life; and for them, as for their coaches, their predestined mediocrity may well be based on methods shunned by the exclusive few. It has always been so. There is no reason to suppose that the age-old concepts and applications will ever alter. The Greeks said so; three thousand years later I see the self-evident truth just as clearly as they did.

The majority of mankind is destined never to be able to discern the meretricious from the true. The hope of mankind must ever remain in the high intelligence, honesty and integrity of its teachers and leaders.

This applies to athletic coaches as well as world leaders and national figures. There is some reason to believe that, athletically, the world has had foisted upon it in this age of factory production, regimentation, and unquestioning authority, regimes of training that must prove inimical to all that tends to develop the gifts of personality and athletic ability in the young athlete.

Therefore, since we are discussing the nature of; and the natural propensities of; the great athlete-to-be – it must be continually emphasized that those disciplined to outside authority, those whose motivations are rooted in the traditional – can never be truly great.

So I seek in my champion something of the quality of the

rebel: one who rebels, instinctively, against the pronouncements of the authoritarian.

I seek in him the intelligent challenger – not the respectful, unthinking acquiescent.

Especially am I unfavourably impressed by any readiness to comply merely because someone has said so: that unthinking, unreflective acceptance of the intellectually dull, or the credulous 'believer' – synonymous terms to me.

So, courage, persistence, inurement to pain and suffering These can be taught – but only by personal example. Merely to *speak* of these concomitants is to present the shadow, the ghost – the *substance* is missing.

The young learn by personal example.

In the end concepts are empty; courage cannot be taught or exemplified by reading it out of books. It is true such examples, related, can be inspiring, but in the end the great coach must be able to exemplify in his own life and personality all that he would teach.

To me it is axiomatic: if he cannot do it he cannot teach it, he can only *talk* about it – and that to me is a vastly different thing.

True teaching is not merely the dissemination of academic learning. If the coach cannot exemplify in his own life that which he teaches, he will fail by just that much to produce great athletes.

Indeed, it can be said that whilst an athlete remains *under* a coach he can never surpass that coach. Put another way, the *greatest* coaches and teachers are never surpassed by their pupils. They only grow old, but the pupils in their turn can flourish as coaches or teachers. Ultimates cannot be added to, nor superlatives superseded.

In the end the 'seeker' finds the teacher. The many merely take what is to hand. If it is 'quantity' one seeks as a teacher, it is best to remain mediocre in method and ambition. That which will attract the exclusive few must in the nature of things repel the many, and vice versa.

So, if you would coach great athletes, be content with a limited few – *the* limited few, who will seek you out. And you, the athlete, will know you have at least some of the seeds of *real* greatness in you when you instinctively reject the 'popular': and are attracted to the teacher rejected by, or, put better, not acceptable to, the many.

The *great* coach must be heterodox. Often he is deemed 'a crank'. More often he is in conflict with authority, officialdom. He rarely enjoys in his best and formative years the recognition that may be later accorded to him, as it invariably is if he is a truly great teacher.

Just as the coach must not be tempted to make too optimistic predictions as to the athlete who rises too quickly in a sudden burst of spectacular performance, so must the athlete not be too ready to accept all that may be presented to him as a sure and certain formula to world-class athletic performance. There just isn't any.

I myself offer nothing but the paraphrased words of a great war-time leader: blood, tears, sweat and suffering. That is the formula to any and all great achievement, at least in the athletic world. I know of no other.

Especially must those who are born with great early gifts be watchful. To be born with early gifts is often to be loaded with the very thing, or qualities, that may eventually undermine us and bring about our discomfiture, even downfall.

How trite and true that the higher we go the harder we fall. The gifted young athlete will do well to remember this when he is being extolled and flattered – as he will be.

It is better, really, to start lowly and slowly, and by one's own efforts and resources to climb to notice, so demanding by one's own efforts the recognitions that may appear, at first, to be tardily accorded.

Those who have Fame thrust upon them are in a most invidious position, since it is almost impossible to envisage the conditions of growth that make for collaterally developed character.

Better far, I repeat, to be one of those perhaps rejected, ignored, to be one of those who, painfully, manfully, struggles ever upwards and eventually *forces* Fame and Fortune, those two dubious characters, maybe, to recognize and accept them.

Nothing can be bestowed. That is, nothing that is worth while. Everything must be earned. That is, everything we can truly appreciate and value. Athletic prowess and sportsmanship – as judged by posterity – proves this.

The truly great ones of the past: the Georges, the Shrubbs, Kohlemainens, Nurmis, Haeggs, McKenleys, Zatopeks, Kutses, and now Elliotts! All athletes of the people – all names typical and representative of hundreds of other names and personalities who have trodden the 'way' before us.

In their beginnings no superior endowments of birth or position, no especial estates, affluence, privileges, even opportunities. Indeed, mostly, exactly the opposite.

Could it be their greatnesses grew out of their lacks? Be glad, those of you who have no preferments – you who are unknown, who start from life's lowest rungs – if you feel the seeds within you be glad, be mightily glad, for yours can be the championships, the records, the fame and the achievement.

But the way may be long – as I have written – wearyingly long; it may be painful, distressingly bitter and painful. But if the seeds are in you all that the greatest have ever achieved can be yours, at least in part.

No athlete started with less endowment of wealth or position, place or education than did Nurmi and Zatopek. Honour them, you heroes, too, of the future, even if it be remote, since these men before you overcame *all* things, conquered *all* things, and in their own times achieved *all* things.

Truly can we make our own destiny, mould or mar the clay that is set.

Go on in faith, you believers in the 'high endeavour'. As our highest Olympic official in Australia wrote to me of and for one of my most promising young athletes recently: Go on – do all the 'right' things – the world, and all that is in it, can be yours.'

Hence, do not overvalue the initial gifts: the elaborate set-up: the great endowment, whether to club or university: the artificial so-called 'cinder tracks' (world records have been set up on grass).

To me these are not the essentials. None of them is necessarily the pre-requisite to great athletic achievements. Nor do they necessarily help in the development of the great athlete of superior performance, personality and character.

Indeed, we have nothing of these things at Portsea. It is true that we enjoy coastal scenery equal to any in our State. It is true we are surrounded with the blue waters of ocean and of sky. But other than that we have nothing: our life is not urban: we live to the music of the sea and the birds, we train to the caresses or inclemencies of beach, sandhill and moor. How much these simplicities and strengths entered the spirits, the souls, of the Perrys, the Macmillans, the Landys, the Stephens, and now the Elliotts and others – no man can truly say – ever completely evaluate.

Maybe these are the true teachers; the real coachings: the School of Simplicity, Strength and Sincerity – to quote a cliché that I once used in my endeavours, many years ago, to inculcate upon the youth gathered around me.

*

1 *A gifted 880 yards runner, with a time of 1:51 at twenty years, and now only twenty-one, apologizing for his recent woeful performances of around two minutes for the 'half', said just that, and meant it – 'Too old'. I was staggered and amazed. He came from the U.S.A. A nonplussed and disillusioned athlete, his coach had not been able, apparently, to help or enlighten him.*

2. *We have no deep or long cultural or athletic history or background.*

3. *Landy also had a most efficient action or technique that made a four minute mile 'look' easy, as it mostly was to J.L. I am one who believes he could have – and should have – run faster. Chataway is such another. Both 'settled' for something less than what they might have accomplished – at least, in my opinion.*

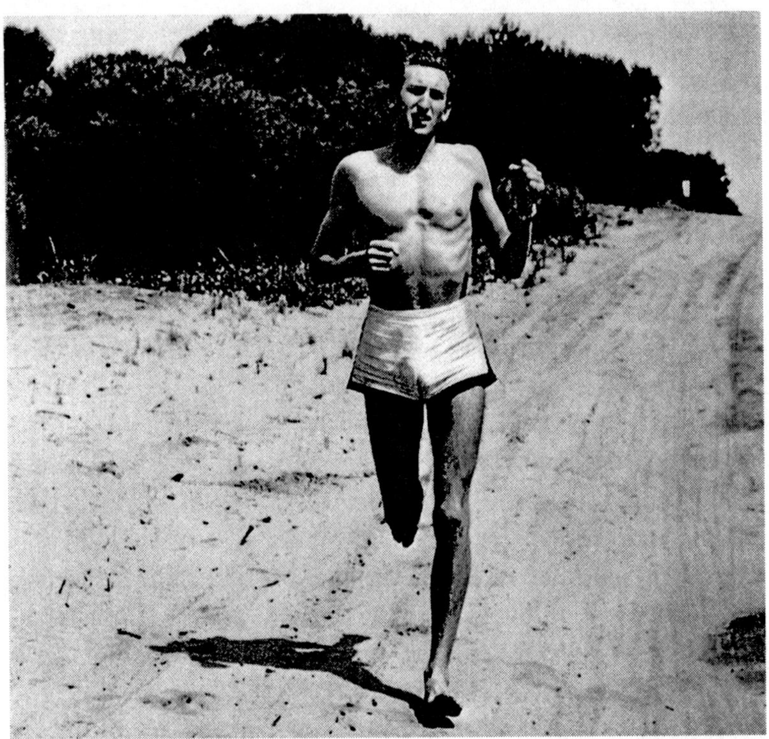

Herb Elliott

The white post at the top of the rise is outside the upper gate of the property. Here is the start and finish of the two major training circuits, the Hall and Stewart.

Elliott is shown in the garb that is adopted for most of the year and all except the coldest or most inclement weather. In the summer, of course, such freedom is ideal. The boys develop naturally and without the customary attitudes that so often cause artificialities and tensions. Note the closed fists even when running easily downhill, the arms being carried high because of the downgrade. The heel landing and absence of strain is so normal and natural as to almost pass unnoticed.

The shrub-like trees are the indigenous ti-tree, with which the area is mostly densely covered. It flowers with a mass of white flowers, giving a similarity to being covered in snow.

We all grow to love the dunes and moors of Portsea.

Herb Elliott

The sand-dunes occur at intervals along our coast intermixed with rugged cliffs and sandy beaches. There is an infinite variety of terrain and scenery. The dunes are clean and free from obstacles calculated to injure the athletes' feet.

The 'boys' – all my athletes are 'our boys' to Nancy (my wife) and myself – train without shoes, some even on the roads and over rocky terrain. Only the veriest newcomer turns up at our grass track with shoes. All our speed work is done bare-footed except when the grass may be dangerously slippery.

The boys enjoy jumping down the face of the dunes from heights as much as twenty feet, often taking tumbles and somersaulting as they fall and roll. This forms an enjoyable part of our free-play and is considered more frolicking than training.

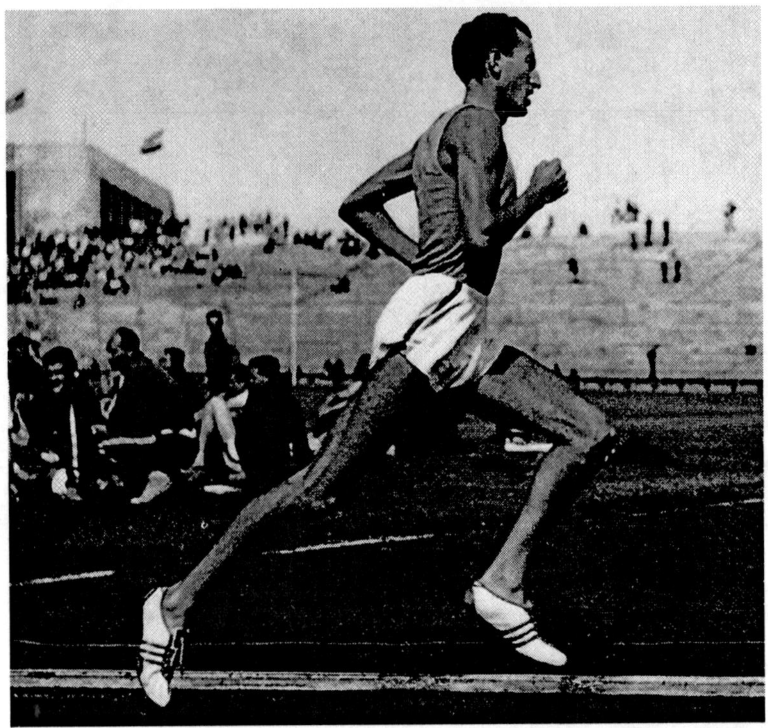

Herb Elliott

In this picture Elliott is a few weeks over his nineteenth birthday, and running his first sub-four minute mile. The absence of spectators, and the casual attitudes of the athletes resting, both indicate that Elliott, as yet, was no sensation. Within a year, he was to pack in 40,000 spectators at some of the biggest athletic stadiums in the world, and cause attendance records to be set up.

Note the effect given by the camera of an elongated leg as Herb drives off his foot. Note, also, the square shoulders, the absence of shoulder sway, the drive of the powerful arms. The foreshortened upper body suggests that the camera was held close to the ground as the picture was taken. Nevertheless it shows the effective technique employed by this master miler. There is no suggestion of ease, as implied by the usual concept of relaxation. Herb did it the hard way. He was strong enough, and resolute enough, to do it that way – successfully.

Herb Elliott

Elliott is shown finishing his first sub-four minute mile race. Being taught to hold his form through the tape, he still drives without the excessive upward throw of the head and abandoned attitudes of the arms so often seen by many otherwise first-class performers. It is also noticeable, as was mostly the case with Herb in his mile races, that no other competitor is close enough to be in the picture.

With his youth, and despite his courage, determination and strength, if anyone suggests that Herb 'breezed' through these races without pain, or 'taking it easy', as so many try to do – to their undoing – they are far from the reality. It is natural for Herb to give of his best: to do his uttermost. A policy I teach and agree with, with all that is possible in my own make-up. At my age I no longer 'kill' myself by driving myself to the uttermost limits.

Chapter 2

The Necessity Of Understanding The Principles And Means Of Gaining Strength And Skills

In the past it was deemed sufficient to run to become a good runner. It was sufficient to take the strength we have and vault, throw the discus, the hammer, the shot.

Now we know differently.

The level of any skill is enhanced when the level of strength is raised. For one thing there are reserves of power that make for continuity of effort (stamina). Where there is greater strength there is a greater measure of control – effort for effort.

I go so far as to say that for superlative performance in the running times of the future, running alone will be found to fall far short of the demands that will make these performances possible.

Indeed in the shorter distances and middle distances running itself may well become secondary to strength conditioning.

When all is said and done, what do we run on? Certainly not the ability to run. The ability to run is rather weakened when we, having run a mile in four minutes, immediately set out to run another mile in the same time.

We say this is impossible – why? The athlete is too weak – we hear it said. Why is he too weak? Merely that the mile in four minutes has drained all his available power for the time being.

Let us find the means of doubling his power and the same athlete will be capable of two miles in 8:I0 or 8:20.

It must be repeated, running alone will not achieve this result. It is obvious we run not on running ability per se but on strength. That the stronger the runner, skill for skill, the faster he will go in his event.

If we view running as a skill, as I suggest, and not as a strength-producing exercise, we get nearer to the modern idea. This is even more readily seen when we think of the jumps, hurdles, field games – all skills, and the athlete's success depends upon the degree of his skill and the rating of his power (strength).

So it seems proved to me that before we can build, or become, a great athlete, we must find a protégé already endowed with great natural strength or find the means of making weaker types stronger.

It has been proved in my experience that athletes inherently weakly by comparison with naturally strong types can be so conditioned that they eventually surpass the naturally strong and achieve performances of superior rating.

Because these 'made' types do not always easily surpass the naturals, the gifted and the inherently strong has led to a disparagement of the ideas as to strength-conditioning. 'There you are,' my opponents say, 'look at this one or that – a world record and never lifted a barbell in his life.' But I say how much has he improved – what did he start from and where did he end? And how much faster may he have run had he been strength-conditioned?

I have in mind a good natural strength-and-ability type in this country, one John Treloar – Empire Games Sprint Champion, finalist in the Olympic Games 100 metres, etc.

At seventeen years of age Treloar ran the '100' in 9:6. He went on to repeat this some twenty-three or twenty-six times in a career lasting some seven years. But he never improved one-tenth of a second on his early schoolboy effort. Was this 'success'? What of his coaches!

Treloar was at the end of his career when I first met him in London. I found there were elements in his starting he was not aware of. He had never been strength-conditioned, and despite years of competition, 'training' and 'coaching'(?) had gained nothing in speed. He did not have the natural strength and stamina to run out a fast 440. It is doubtful if either muscles or lungs or heart were conditioned sufficiently to permit a two-minute 880 or a 4:3 mile.

Now we know differently to this. Hogan in Australia is just such another. With an amazing early burst of speed, he has neither the strength nor the will to run out a fast 220, in the order of a sub twenty-one-second furlong. This again indicates an inherent defect in the athlete and a grievous lack in the coaching ability by those with whom he has been associated. Both the Australians I cite could have been greater.

It is true that it is easier to get more startling results in the middle-distance field. But I contend there were no appreciable results at all in the case of Treloar and Hogan.

It is relatively easy, I have found, to get a lad of twenty years, and after a year or so of ordinary training and competition, for me to so strengthen him that he will move from his customary 4:50 mile to a 4:30 mile in one season.

His co-athlete, unconditioned, remains, sometimes for ever, on the 4:50 mile level. I could quote dozens of examples in my personal experience, perhaps the most world-renowned being that of John Landy. Landy has placed on record that had he not met me, he would never have even considered running faster than 4:30 for the mile.

At nineteen years of age – with a 4:37 mile best – Landy was a normally exercised but non-strength-conditioned youth.

He was, as most are, weak in the upper body and arms. He was a 'leg' runner – having more than ordinarily powerful legs. His extensive training over many years developed his upper leg muscles to a degree that gave him the largest thighs – body weight for body weight and height – of any class athlete I have seen.

Landy's upper body was strengthened with a sixty-pound dumbbell, which he used for all exercises. In addition he practised chinning the bar, body presses, etc.

Within a year he had increased his arm and upper body strength very considerably and was in the upper three or four in strength of my group of ten or twelve at Portsea that year.

But he never became exceptionally strong in the arms and upper body, and remained throughout his career a 'leg' runner of the 'pacer' type, and was quite unable to exert himself in the thrashing violent way essential to hard, fast finishers. As a great runner, Landy failed by just that much. He is known to have wished he had strengthened his upper body more.

I could not persuade him to do so in those early formative years. He bought from me a sixty-pound dumbbell. Macmillan, Stephens, Perry, Warren and all others of my group of that time either acquired full barbell sets around 150–lb. or used them in gymnasiums.

All these athletes quickly replaced the champions of the day – in one year, actually – once they were strength-conditioned by the means that I had proved in my own personal experience.

What were those means?

Before outlining the means it may be better to state briefly how I arrived at the means and methods that I advocate.

Following the usual trend of an ordinary citizen in my early forties, my health and strength showed marked signs of serious deterioration.

Through circumstances which I shall not detail in this account, I became interested in exercising. This took the form of walking – especially in mountains – running, swimming and diving, horizontal bar work and weight lifting.

As my strength increased due to these various activities, I found my level of performance greatly enhanced, until I was able to perform, in most activities, at a higher level of effort at fifty years of age than at any previous time in my life.

Able in the beginning to lift barely sixty pounds overhead, after a year or so of strenuous work I was enabled to lift overhead almost double that weight. All other abilities increased proportionately.

From being a sceptic, as to the need or use of the barbell, I became an enthusiastic convert.

I found that the charges of 'muscle bound', 'slow you up' 'weaken your heart', 'unnatural', all were without foundation or sense.

I found in my own experience a strength, speed, agility and stamina higher than ever at any time in my life previously. At fifty-five years of age I was sprinting faster, probably, than ever in my life before. My ability to run five miles and ten miles was certainly increased at fifty to what it was at twenty years of age. My recorded times proved it.

As I developed my ideas, I almost entirely abandoned the orthodox and traditional way of training for running – that is, running on level ground, tracks, etc., walking or running up hills slowly, i.e. conserving energy, and trying to become faster and stronger by repeated efforts on the track.

In place of these customary athletic activities I 'trained' by long walks in our mountains, covering such distances as 220 miles in ten days – as an example – carrying a rucksack with food, tent, etc., and recording eventually 200 miles covered in five days, two of the five rest, or non-active, days.

Instead of running on hard surfaces I commenced running on soft surfaces, until now much of our training in the winter conditioning period is done running on the soft, dry, loose sand of our Australian beaches. Also we run up the steep sides of sand dunes, and when in urban districts select the steepest hills in parks or streets and run as vigorously up them as we are able.

Such activities use the body as a resistance and I hold that for the development of the legs and lungs and heart little or no other exercise for the legs is necessary. But the strength development of the torso, in particular the pectorals, back, stomach and arms, are not catered for sufficiently with the running, no matter how vigorous or sustained, and in our conditioning work almost as many hours are applied to strength-conditioning with the barbell and other gymnasium apparatus as in running itself. All I can say is, in regard to many weakly types that have been trained by these methods, the results have been startling, not the least being Landy and Stephens, neither particularly strongly endowed types in the beginning.

Again, I do not feel this introductory treatise is the place to go into the details of strength-conditioning except to repeat briefly that I believe in the intensive approach – that what we do, we do with all our heart and soul. Lift and strive, blow and grunt – whether on the sandhill or with the barbell.

There are those who recoil from herculean efforts – who consider possible ruptures and strains as sufficient deterrents, and over-exertion the cause of weak hearts.

I hold that those who approach their exercise and goals in this way will fall short in their final endeavours and results of what they might have achieved, no matter if the achievement was a world record.

CHAPTER 3

The importance of the naturalistic technique, especially in relation to posture, movement and the physical development of the athlete

If a close study of animals, children and primitives is made, certain aspects of movement become apparent. At this juncture it may be helpful to outline how I arrived at my ideas and opinions on, as well as realizing the importance of; posture and technique.

Coming back to running at the age of forty-five years after more than twenty years' non-participation, I brought three factors to the subject and study:

1. A lively interest and a capacity for analysis and deduction.
2. An intense scepticism that applied to all aspects of our education and culture, political and religious – a growing contempt and intense dislike for most of the things other people valued.
3. A trained scientific approach, based on the electrical sciences. Also I had made a study, if only an elementary one, of most other sciences, including medicine and disease.

This, then, was the man and mind that became interested enough to do some thinking about, and research into, the art of movement and posture-running.

I soon discovered that most or all the accepted opinions and teachings were, to say the least, doubtful. Little appeared valid, either in 'how to run' or how to train for superlative effort.

The writings of three men of those days, however, could not be dismissed in any cavalier fashion. These men were Arthur Newton, George Hackenschmidt and Bob. Hoffman. The first had revolutionized distance running and had much that was new to contribute. The second was a strength and wrestling phenomenon, who had wittingly or unwittingly dropped upon the only true approach, mental and physical, to exercise and sport. Hoffman contributed the technique of systematic conditioning for strength.

Basically, my attitudes and ideas are rooted in the fundamentals expounded by these three giants in their particular spheres, all of whom I later met personally.

Because of their stature in their particular fields, their ideas have been beyond the understanding and appreciation of the many who always were, and always will be, attracted to the mediocre, the meretricious, the clap-trap or the purely charlatan, although the weight-lifting world largely functions on the ideas of Hoffman.

Newton taught the importance of consistent training: the daily balanced effort, the high aim. He made little or no contribution to two other vital factors, ailment or posture.

In regard to posture it is meet to observe that although he accepted his own postural running gift as normal, he was undoubtedly one of the most gifted movers that I have ever seen. His world records were as equally based on his gift of posture and movement, as on his training, which was of the extreme extensive order. Newton, as is the case with all real champions, was born with gifts and merely fulfilled his destiny.

In the case of Hackenschmidt, he was born with gifts of mind and physique of an exceptional order. In his youth he attracted the notice of the leading medical man of his country,

Russia. This medical man had attained to the eminence of court physician to the Czar, and it was he who, taking Hackenschmidt into his home, provided him with the gymnasium, barbells and education that later made this man one of the greatest colossi in the realms of mind and body the world has known.

It may be centuries before the abilities of Hackenschmidt are fully understood and appreciated, since his teachings are far beyond the capacity and imagination of most of the coaches and trainers, indeed minds, of our day.

I have no hesitation, then, in saying that little of what follows can be properly claimed as original thought on my part.

If I contribute anything, it is merely that I advance the matter a little further, just as Newton, the physicist, advanced the knowledge of Galileo – Einstein of Newton. Indeed, in this respect, whilst modesty should compel me to remain silent, the necessity to convince others demands the statement that Newton, the athlete, once said that I carried on the matter of running where he left off; whether this be true or merely the generous statement of a singularly gifted man, I do not know, but it *is* true that, age for age, I was enabled to run faster than Newton, since I *did* carry his technique and training a further step forward, incorporating a certain *intensity* in place of the emphasis on extensive training.

Summed up, Newton taught me the value of posture and systematic effort (training) and an utter lack of respect for persons and performances – that records were merely goals to be achieved. Hackenschmidt taught me the importance of strength, how it is developed and the power of the deep personality.

Essential, then, is a study of the work of these two exceptional athletes – athletes whose feats are never likely to be surpassed if we view them in relation to their contemporaries, since they were as far ahead of their contemporaries as a jet engine is of the orthodox type petrol engine.

I lived with Newton for some two or three months and have

talked with Hackenschmidt, but my basic knowledge of their work was gained in each case from their writings. Much of the work of both these men is out of print unfortunately, but Bob Hoffman of the U.S.A., a leader for decades, and in the weight-lifting and conditioning field on world-class levels, has reprinted and kept available to this day one of Hackenschmidt's earliest and simplest works.

I could wish my good friend Bob, who also contributed in no mean way to my sum of knowledge through his own writings and work, would extend the publication of 'Hack's' books, since the principles are as true today as when first promulgated, well over half a century ago.

So, finding the athletic literature of the day had little to say upon the vital matters of posture, movement, diet or championship performance other than in the works of Newton, Hackenschmidt and Hoffman, I fell to many years of personal research and experimentation.

Firstly, I turned to all and any literature that dealt with the anatomy, both physiological and artistic. I studied every subject that could even remotely be thought to be associated with movement and athletic performance, mentally, physically and spiritually (if this latter can be separated from the first two).

I myself took up weight-lifting both as a conditioner and as a sport, but owing to my age and marked limitations was wise never to compete officially.

I returned to the simple gymnastic feats of my youth, handstands and the horizontal bar; I dropped tennis and golf and returned to running, swimming, diving and mountain walking. Incidentally, in doing these things I put the clock back exactly one quarter of a century, regained my lost youth, the zest for living and enjoyed performances, mostly but not all, exceeding anything ever attained to in the years supposedly called our 'prime'.

For those who are statistically minded and like 'evidence',

my studies took me through some 200 serious textbooks or so. I believe I covered the whole modern gamut of science, philosophy and all allied subjects in some way – both serious and cursory.

Parallel with all this was some ten years of extensive experimentation on my own body (and mind, since we cannot separate them).

I tried every possible variation in human perambulation, every type of posture, movement and adaptation. I ran with a slithering shuffle. I ran with the highest possible prance and knee lift. I ran bent, erect, long stride, chopped stride. I ran fast and slow, on heels, on toes, head in every possible position – arms thrashing; arms immobilized.

Out of the ceaseless welter of experiment, trial and error came, my 'set' ideas: I feel there is no further to go. There *is* a correct posture: it applies to *all*. There *is* a proper and true way of moving the arms and hands and fingers: its variations (and there are many) apply to *all*. There is a true and proper way to move the legs, and land on the feet – 100-yarder or 100-miler: the principles of movement apply equally to both.

To me these attitudes are beyond argument, since they are demonstrable in my own person as well as others. Indeed, much of what I claim was known to all the 'greats' such as George, Shrubb, Nurmi, Zatopek, McKenley, to name a few of the most prominent. It is doubtful if any of these knew *all*.

If I have a useful purpose in writing this book, it may be to correlate all that was known and expounded by these athletic prodigies and to add, perhaps, my own conclusions.

My earliest studies were those of animals. I studied the skeleton of the great racehorse Phar Lap, as well as devoting many hours, for many years, watching and running alongside our greatest racehorses. I learnt much.

Amongst other things I learnt from the study of the racehorse was that they all moved *exactly* similarly: that a silhouette of one going fast fitted exactly into a silhouette of another – extent of leg-throw – movement of legs – head and neck angles and relationships – all identical. Whether heavily built or lightly, long in the legs or not so long, tall or short. Another factor of interest was that whilst the horse 'appeared' to bound along with violent and convulsive efforts, in actual fact all was so rhythmical that the head and back merely moved in a relatively gentle undulatory motion that made it possible, unless the horse swerved or stumbled, to provide a truly 'armchair' ride for the diminutive riders perched (apparently) so precariously upon their mounts' backs.

Other facts and factors were brought out, but these are outside the scope of this volume: such as the impression of 'power', absence of strain and the ability to expend completely all their energy, mostly leaving little to finish with as they approached the winning post.

The subsidence of extreme effort into relaxed movement, and matters relating to warming up (pre-race activity) and warming down (the most farcical of the many modern teachings), all these and others would require a further volume to adequately describe and comment upon.

Parallel with this study of the horse was the study of the movements of gazelles, and the higher apes, panthers and leopards, in particular.

Without some such study, or teachings, no athlete or coach can even hope to aspire, understand, or 'feel' what is perfect human posture and movement (perambulation). The great and finished (perfected) athlete of the future will be seen to have the relaxed power, grace and resiliency of the blood horse both in walking and running – especially the absence of 'haste' in his movements. He will have the 'up'–ness, that 'apparent' faculty of being *over* the ground, that the gazelle suggests in its stance and movement, and the litheness and resolute ferocity that is in the posture and movement of the leopard and panther, whether at rest, walking or moving at full speed. With maturity he will have the detached, impersonal 'Kingness' of the lion.

My first studies of animals was made on the movements of the anthropoid apes.

Indeed, at that time I based my running movements, as well as walking and normal posture, upon what I observed.

This resulted in no attempt at all to impose 'style'. Running was mostly an effortless shuffle: no knee lift at slow paces, dangling arms – no shoulder or body movements.

The style of the marathon runner Gordon Stanley, Australian champion, and record- holder, was largely based in this low foot carriage, short-striding style. It proved ineffective against the freer movements of the Englishman Holden in the Empire Games, Auckland.

Further studies of the antelope and gazelle suggested there was a means of running lightly *over* the ground rather than upon it, and this is true.

How to acquire this means was not easy to ascertain. I found it a 'gift of nature' in men like Newton, who had it *par excellence.*

It is not easily taught, since it rests in certain natural approaches, or mental states inherent in the personality. But knowledge that induces the mental states can be taught even if the posture cannot.

For I have learnt this one thing – no one can be taught a true running posture or movement. The mind and personality of the athlete must be educated or altered so that his bodily movements conform to new aspects and approaches. If the athlete is merely taught to do this or do that he will impose further strains and tensions upon his organism and bring about conditions more disposed to hamper his progress than add to his possibilities.

But the ability to move speedily, lightly and effectively in that detached, upright posture of the gazelle can be understood and the concepts, once explained and adopted, can influence an athlete to his very great advantage in performance, especially in the events concerned with levitation – the high jump, pole vault, hurdles and the long jump.

A study of the movements of the horse drew the conclusions that no effort must be made to stride: that the stride is truly related to strength and posture.

It is evident that an athlete's fundamental movements are not based in the naturalistic technique when he complains he 'cannot run slowly'. That his attempts to amble with a short stride of a foot or two are a series of tensed slow motion longer strides of a yard or more. An athlete who cannot run as slowly as two miles per hour is certainly one who does not run naturally and is sure to fail to reach great athletic heights because of his limitation.

This type of athlete will not be able to let his arms hang naturally, since all his consciousness is fixed in his legs and his arms are *carried*, rather than used, whether he runs fast or slowly.

The study of the movements, the litheness and power of the panther and leopard gave rise to further aspects. Here we have the pose and movements of the killer. With the gazelle and the horse we have the uplifted movements of the animal who has made flight his chief aspect or prerogative.

But the down-to-earth power and speed of the leopard, cheetah, panther, jaguar and tiger is of another order.

Both these aspects, attitudes and primary approaches will be found in the most successful athletes of our day. Undoubtedly Iharos had the natural uplift and movement of the gazelle, Zatopek the galloping power of the horse, and in the youth Elliott we have the movements and the mental ferocity in his approach to running of the leopard and panther. Elliott is a typical killer type.

So much for animals. What of humans?

Contrary to what I had expected to find, I found that the

Chinese, the people of India, the Arab and those of Northern Africa and the Middle East had nothing to contribute whatever.

Where, because of low levels of modern civilization, I had expected to find a 'closer to earth', naturalistic state, I found, because of their age–long culture and civilization, these peoples had moved farther from the purely natural and instinctive than even the majority of Northern Europeans, the so-called 'whites'.

Indeed, many 'whites' were basically less civilized, more primitive, than their coloured brothers, if we judged on naturalistic posture and movements. That this is true is beyond question, and the relatively poor performance of these people of ancient cultural lineage is due to the fact that they, more than most, have lost the natural ability to move and live instinctively in a purely animal fashion.

Their lack of athletic ability is not, then, solely due to lack of spirit, courage or knowledge of training or the ability to train arduously and consistently, as is so commonly imputed.

There is one exception – the Negro.

Perhaps he has remained closer to the true primitive in his culture in Africa and his recent, anthropologically speaking, transference to North America has not been of sufficient duration to deprive him of his natural movements and instinctive relaxation.

I definitely feel his racial success in the sports he succeeds in, running and boxing, particularly, are due to his retaining the spontaneous and instantaneous responses of an organism still very close to the purely natural, both in flight and fight.

I encourage my athletes to return to these natural and primitive approaches and states if they wish to succeed as athletes, at least on the topmost level.

To help us in our studies there has providentially been provided, one is tempted to say, a race, almost extinct, that provides the key to the art and business of efficient natural perambulation. I refer to the Australian aborigine.

Unique in the world as to their Stone Age culture, and, until

200 years or so ago, their isolated environment, this people has evolved with cultural aspects positively unique, at least in my experience.

Especially is this true of those who have evolved in the central and the far north-western area of the continent. Here we find developed to the highest degree, natural capacities without equal in any other race.

Completely removed from time immemorial, from the culture of Europe, Asia, Africa and the Americas, this race of *Homo sapiens* has evolved with an attitude to life and living without parallel in the world today.

The aborigine has evolved a culture that has no sense of divine guilt or punishment. He has no sense of property or any acquisitive sense. In his culture all are truly equal as to goods and possessions, if any. He has no aristocracy, no hierarchy, no government and, in our view, no religion.

He is therefore, in his purely natural environment, without any sense of guilt or shame, and lives in a state of natural nakedness.

Physically, he has evolved with the leanest of physiques, especially his legs, being almost without shape or muscle by normal European shapes and standards.

His posture is perfectly upright and is gazelle-like and uplifted. He moves over the ground with movements that are different to the movements based in the posture of Europeans, Asians and to some extent Africans, although some of these latter, as do the Tierra del Fuegians and South Sea Islanders and Maoris, approach more nearly to the movements of these true Australians.

They stand absolutely erect – heads carried in perfect alignment with the spine, which is nearly straight, and the feet approach the ground swung forward by the legs, not unlike the movements of the gazelle in uprightness and the easy grace of blood stock horse.

It is true, 'contact with civilization soon modifies these attributes and graces, as does the acquirement of the Christian religion with its shames and guilts.

But the true primitives retain these age-long inherited factors that differentiate them: they walk and run differently to any other race, and, I have observed, run fast and efficiently, although as primitives they are unable to understand the reason for racing nor do they derive an incentive from the thought of prestige, prizes or money, as do their other-than-Australian brothers.

In running there is a noticeable absence of knee-lift, the legs being lifted only high enough for the purpose and speed aimed at. This knee lift, or absence of it, is governed by the downward extended-arm carriage. No attempt is made to crook the elbow or throw the hands and arms across the chest.

The downward thrusting arms, almost straight, are thrown vigorously forward and slightly across the body, thus keeping the legs low and forcing a long, low, effective and strength-saving stride.

With little or no calf muscle and lightly built thighs, their speed is amazing, but the mentality lacks the drives and incentives that motivate us. Hence racing is purposeless. This is hardly the basis for Gold Medal winning at Olympics. When their minds are conditioned to European standards and culture, then much that is the normal and natural inheritance of these savages – all of whom are kings in their own right, with a truly regal bearing – much of this is lost and the athletic performance suffers by so much, although much agility and speed and natural posture is still retained.

So my observations carried me along until I realized that the perfect athlete evidenced something of the upright stance and running movements of the aborigine and the gazelle, the power and drive of the race horse, the litheness and killer instinct of the tiger, leopard, panther and jaguar.

How to encourage and incorporate these attributes into a youth brought up in an ordinary family in a civilized country is not easy. They can be more easily spoken about – taught– than acquired.

Indeed, any adaptation to them, any changes or enhanced abilities, *must* come from within the athlete himself.

As soon as the athlete is told to, or he feels he is expected to, assume certain postures and movements, he only acquires tensions, strains and unnatural postures and movements.

Mostly his case is made worse than hitherto, and if his conditioning and training is not added to, his level of performance can conceivably fall, rather than rise, through the injunctions of coaches telling him to relax, land on his feet this way or that, or move his arms in this fashion or the other.

Indeed, no such orders must be given.

Instead, the athlete must be educated to a certain attitude. It must be explained to him how the gazelle looks out on life, how it would feel, why it is so erect and has the extraordinary capacity for bounding and for speed.

The same ideas and education apply to the horse, the jaguars and leopards. Unless he can feel the ferocity and aloof intensity of these animals it is useless for him to be expected to run as they do – as he can.

I have mentioned the apes last. It was some years after I had adopted the low shuffling movements of the apes as efficient that I realized what the ape lacks. He lacks 'awareness' – awakened consciousness. Not that humans are endowed with a high degree of either; they are not, but their mental approach is an uplifted one in comparison with the mental states of the ape.

The ape is the acme of natural or unenlightened movement; the aborigine the apex of natural self-conscious manhood and movement, upright and fearless. The highest level of human development incorporates the aspects of the aborigine, but superimposes upon it the ferocity and singleness of purpose of the carnivorous animal combined with the idealism, incentives and appreciation of the rewards and prestige associated with competition between human beings.

If we study the movements of the child from three or four years to eight or ten years we will see, in most cases, free uninhibited movements – no tensions, no poses, no false assumptions. But from puberty, in particular, the growing young man acquires the postures, attitudes and movements of those deemed to be his peers.

He is taught to do things this way or that – even when not taught he observes the methods and movements of those he admires, and copies them, mostly exactly.

If these examples are of a poor order, despite any natural gifts the lad may have, he will tend to remain on much the same level as those he copies and admires.

Thus it is that, when coaches lack knowledge, character and great aspirations, the level of performance from that club, school, university or country will tend to sink to the level of that coach or coaches.

And when men of greater calibre arise, the level in that place will rise irrespective of the material offering, which is much the same in any country or race. The remarkable adaptability of the human race makes this assertion reasonable.

So when coaches, mentors and teachers impose concepts as to posture and movement upon their pupils or athletes, the result of these accepted or imposed ideas and states is to cause tensions that inhibit free performance. The object of the teacher is not to impose a technique by rule or direction, but to free the pupil or athlete from the conditioned responses that the body has usually adopted by the acceptance of false standards, beliefs and ideas in our civilization. These are all mental first.

The odd ones, who are not normally conditioned by our civilization – who continue to function in a natural and instinctive manner – these youths usually perform athletically on a higher level than their fellows, and because of this are termed 'naturals'.

They, more often than not, spend most of their time resisting the imposed ideas of their teachers and coaches. As they successfully resist these ideas, or find superior teachers or coaches, so they tend to excel in their later life as athletes.

Many of them defy all orthodox concepts, as did the great Australian batsman, Bradman, with his cross-bat technique.

Indeed, the evolution of any sport and athletics generally is the story of the rejection of the orthodox and the finding of new concepts and methods; the most recent and successful being the technique in the shot put of O'Brien, the throwing of the javelin by the Spaniard and the eight-foot high jump of the gymnast. These latter two, marked improvements in results aimed for, are rejected merely because they are heterodox in technique. If throwing the javelin further or jumping higher is an objective, it is ridiculous to impose restrictions as to technique and limitations upon the advanced experimenter and superior performance. This is the attitude of the conservative, the traditionalist, of he who is in opposition at all times to the experimentalist and innovator.

It is the same old story of the man who aims at control (officialdom) and the man who aims at research and excelling.

It is the advancing athlete who carries technique and performance forward, as have the high jumpers, the rules always having to be amended from time to time to keep abreast of performance.

Never did the rules free an athlete, or advance his desire to excel. Most rules are limiting, many retrogressive; all suggest control, are repressive and aim at conditioning an athlete to something less, rather than freeing him to become something more.

Their justification is claimed as essential. There are some of us who doubt this. Many of the rules will not stand intelligent unbiased examination.

I have referred to the new technique devised by O'Brien, the Spanish javelin thrower and the high jumper.

I now have in mind the futile rules of the walker and the limitations imposed by the circles of the hammer thrower and discus thrower – both arbitrary limitations, imposed in place of the line or board, which limits the take-off place of the long jumper and the javelin thrower.

Custom demands these false and arbitrary confining circles. Common sense would free the thrower to adopt his own movements, both spatial and involuntary, to get the best results.

Even the lanes of the circular track impose limitations, advantages and disadvantages upon the athlete, and which are in no way compensated by the draw for lanes. That even applies to the 100 metres straight.

I am not suggesting solutions, but I am criticizing the approach of the rule-maker – the controller, he who usually rejoices in his position and power to the detriment of the athlete. But because I do not suggest solutions, it does not mean that solutions do not exist. It does mean, in my view, that this book is not the place to suggest solutions of this nature – and also that others may have solutions and not necessarily the writer only.

This criticism can also be directed at the starter, who so often demands a fixity, or absence of movement, that borders on the ludicrous, when applied to distance events. A lack of the imagination and understanding derived from personal experience as a competitor is the chief cause of the attitudes of the official starter.

Herb Elliott

Here Elliott is seen even more remorseless, determined and dominating, with as fine a disregard for his own feelings or sufferings as one could wish to see. He was in the race to win, not merely to compete. It has been only an occasional carelessness and a temporary disregard for the need for rest, and training, that has made it possible for Elliott to have been beaten in the few races as a senior in which he has not finished first. There have been races as a senior in which he has not finished first. There have been races, and the two-mile world record run of Thomas' at Dublin, when Elliott finished second, where had has been beaten on his merits on the day. This race followed the day after his world-shattering 3.54.5 mile time. But Thomas also ran fast – 3.58.6 – and set the first two lap speeds in that race, then went on to run his world record twenty-four hours afterwards.

Thomas had been trained by me to become supreme in the three mile. He evidently was able, in personality, to link up the 'two' with the three mile.

Exercising at Portsea

This picture is indicative of the athletes as well as the work that goes on at Portsea.

The athletes are: Ray Smith, Olympic walker, standing. Nearest to me, Jon Bosisto, a good four forty yards hurdler, but not quite of international standard. John Keenan, at fifteen years of age a gifted junior, but who has not yet fulfilled the high destiny that it was hoped may have been his. With a 4:17 mile at seventeen years of age, he is one of our best-performed juniors. Ian Beck, of South Australia, a State senior representative whilst still a junior at school. Beck is also slow in fulfilling his early promise, but may yet hit world headlines. Maurice Bevan, a youth who, at sixteen years of age, presented himself unannounced at Portsea, newly arrived from England, and said, 'I have come!' meaning he had arrived and expected to be turned into a world champion – like that! And on the end of the line, Herb Elliott.

CHAPTER 4

The recognition that anything that is inhibited, mechanical, regimented, done under imposed duress or direction, even that which may be thought to be self-imposed – anything at all that is not free, out-flowing, out-pouring, instinctive and spontaneous – in the end stultifies the objectives, limits the progress, and destroys the possibility of a completely and fully developed personality – athlete and man.

It may be advisable to draw a simple comparison as to what all the above does mean.

Let us consider a person, directed as to how he shall speak, what he shall say, and asked to deliver this message, perhaps one on which he lacks conviction – such a person is self-conscious, usually stammers in his articulation, hesitates, omits, repeats and in many ways is obviously not 'perfect', that is, convincing, sincere, natural and spontaneous in his approach and diction.

Let us contrast such a person with the throbbing outpouring of the canary; the blackbird; the thrush. Here the very soul of the bird throbs and vibrates in an outpouring that is inconceivable when we measure its song against the bird itself its throat and lung power.

So do most athletes stumble and deny. They try hard enough but mostly succeed in a poor and laborious manner to do something that should be done with ease, efficiency and grace.

This subject, then, and the matter contained in it, is more for the coach than the athlete.

I take my stand on two counts:

1. If the coach cannot do it, he cannot 'teach' it – only talk about it.
2. If he, the coach, is a 'little' man, he will strive to remain in authority, retain control over his athletes, dominate them by assuming a superior position to the athlete.

Let us investigate the – 'If the coach cannot do it, he cannot teach it' proposition first.

It is true such a coach can 'presume to know'. He can claim to have seen, heard and read. But no thing that cannot be proved in our personal experience can ever be completely true for us, no matter how we pretend to conviction. And such an attitude never fools those destined to be truly great.

I have known in my own experience too many good athletes who have tolerated the teachings of their coaches when at school, but nevertheless knew instinctively that they were wrong, where they were wrong and later proved conclusively that this was so.

Indeed, immediately I find that an athlete is a 'conformer', a respecter of authority, who is diligent in doing exactly as he is told, just as soon do I know such an athlete is limited in his capacity and never can become truly great. If he is not in my 'camp', such a one is not to be feared. Experience has taught me this – it is not merely an intellectual assumption (I speak of the local scene – not international).

Most coaches are forced by their vocation, both professional and amateur, to assume a knowledge based outside their own experience – that is, upon hearsay; what some other authority is said to have found. That must go for the reader of this exposition. If he cannot repeat in his own experience all the matters

I deal with, he must fall back on 'I believe' – rather than I am. Faith, rather than knowledge of a personally experienced nature; intellectual concepts rather than 'feeling'. By just that much must he fall short of being the 'complete coach' and teacher.

Thus athletics is mostly a case of the blind leading the blind, of authority and direction. Where the coaching level is high, good athletes will tend to be produced in a steady stream.

Never was it truer than in athletics – by their deeds do we know them. Add to this that a man is known by the company he keeps – or his particular set of beliefs, affiliations, admirations and the like.

Let it be said that I have few or none, that my own attitude has mostly been autocratic, independent, suspicious of authority and devoted to personal experience as the Key.

To have any other approach, to me, is to leave oneself open to being fooled, and to appear ridiculous in the eyes of those who truly know – a very limited band – always.

Therefore the effort of the coach, as the athlete, must be in personal experience, suffering and sacrifice if he is 'to know'.

Unfit, inactive coaches can never fully know. They may be able to help; indeed, better teachers and coaches are usually not available, so schools and clubs just must make do with the level of coaching material available to them.

To me, to be a first-class coach is still to be a first-class athlete; although age may have made it impossible to compete equally with youth, such a coach will be a peer amongst his contemporaries, both physically and mentally, in deed and performance, upon the track or his specialized events.

In truth, if he cannot do it, he cannot be expected to gain the conviction of the man who can. He can but repeat what he believes to be true; and he will fail by just that much as against his more gifted fellow who does, then calls upon his daily personal experience as found in himself, rather than what others tell him.

The second category of coaches, mentors and teachers can never hope at all for truly big success.

An athlete can only become as big as his coach. After that he will leave him. This is too commonplace an experience to gainsay contradiction.

Every athlete who ever came to me, left another coach, or teacher, to do so.

The 'big' man has no need to fall back on direction, dictation, orders or threats. His own life will be his evidence and power of conviction, his authority. To be truly great, one's own life must be a personal masterpiece.

Such a coach will painstakingly explain – he will demonstrate in his own person that which he is teaching, even if it be but in little. For example, if the coach is teaching an athlete how to drive over the last lap of a hard and fast mile he must be able, irrespective of age, to be able, himself; to drive over the last furlong, last 100 yards, or even only the last few yards, but he will be able to drive and to demonstrate in his own person what he is talking about. It is useless for him to merely talk about it; what someone else did. If he can do it, even in little, the athlete will recognize this and will understand him, and, with his youth and strength, advance the attitudes and convictions of his coach to both vindicate himself as an athlete and his respect and belief in his coach.

Indeed, I can envisage the aged coach – not able to run more than a few yards, perhaps, but still able to carry conviction by his power of personality and his physically demonstrable movements.

The 'little' man can be detected by his 'do this or that' attitude, and by his reluctance or inability to give a convincing reason for his direction and statements.

Such a man resorts to authority other than himself when pushed. He quotes so and so as the great authority. He will punish, threaten, and will tend to keep himself separate from his charges. He will be 'The Coach'; 'The Boss'; the representative of authority, power and discipline. Such a man would not succeed in the highest plane of endeavour with animals, much less young humans.

What, then, is required in the coach that he inculcates free expression and the acme of high performance?

First of all, he must not assume a position of authority. He is best not being employed in his capacity. He should be there as coach because of his present demonstrable ability and performances, that in themselves inspire confidence and conviction in his athletes.

Young athletes are quick to appraise the efforts of their coach.

A coach who, at forty, can run a mile in five minutes, as he should, will carry more conviction than a world-record holder for that distance. The loyalties of his charges will ensure that.

But if he cannot, he can never enjoy the respect and conviction that he otherwise may.

Remember, please, that the coaches may readily convince, even fool, the young as they sometimes do. But they never fool the older man of superior knowledge, experience or attainments.

In the end, we are hoist with our own petards, live and die according to our own intrinsic worth.

Who, then, are the judges? We judge ourselves by our own performances, abilities and what we produce. A poor tree can never produce first-class fruit, nor poor land a good crop.

Whenever, as in Hungary, first-class performers are thrown up, let it be said that somewhere behind the scenes are first-class, knowledgeable personalities and coaches.

When they pass away, as they seem to do, that country will tend to sink back to mediocrity and another country come into prominence. We have seen it happen in our experience as to Finland, Poland, Sweden, Belgium, England – indeed most or all countries.

The inability of the U.S.A. to produce a series of world-class distance runners is not due to the college system but to the lack of clubs for graduates – they would spontaneously come into being if there were in the U.S.A. coaches in sufficient numbers, personally experienced in distance running and with an understanding and enthusiastic approach. We know on the testimony of the handful of good distance runners in the U.S.A. that this is not so. The coaches, in general, just do not exist apparently, to produce the desired results.

When this factor is remedied, if it ever be remedied, then the U.S.A., with its numbers, climate and resources, will equal or excel the world in distance performers as it has in its own traditionally successful events.

I hold that the athlete must never be asked to conform or train according to a set schedule. He is best developing his ability in line with the Swedish concepts of speed-play, called Fartlek.

There is a tendency today to look upon speed-play in the fields, woods and parklands as outmoded. This is to be regretted, since the track is no place for developing the natural athlete, the set-out track itself being an artificial development, both as to its lack of variety and the usual hardness of its surface.

We may have to race upon it, but we should in no wise be compelled to train exclusively upon such an unnatural medium.

Nothing is more conducive to the production of artificial gaits, false movements, tensions and an untrue self-conscious approach as the continual use of the track as the sole medium of conditioning and training.

The modern track, as the modern spiked shoe, are both artificial and not found in Nature, and the over-use of both, in the end, must inhibit the full development of the athlete.

I work along these lines.

A lad comes to me, always uninvited: I hold that the teacher and the athlete instinctively find each other, even if thousands of miles apart in the beginning, if need be.

Furthermore, I am never impressed by, nor do I feel favourable to, the young athlete upon his first introduction, no matter what reputation or promise accompanies him. Too often I have been misled by both as to ultimates and absolutes. I never count my chickens before they are hatched, nor my 'champion' before he has 'arrived'.

The 'not-done' is the unproved, to me. In that regard belief is not true, only faith – and faith is the substance of things unproved. When proved it is certainty; established fact; knowledge; experience. Up to then it is suspect; that goes for faith in anyone or any doctrine with me.

Further, I feel that no man can reasonably have complete faith in another, much less a doctrine or dogma. The only true convictions I really have are those that rest in myself, my own powers, my own personality.

To me, this statement is simple, obvious and axiomatic. To others, no doubt, it is autocratic and offensive. To this I am completely indifferent – as we should be.

If, after my unfavourable first acquaintance with him, the athlete, or would-be athlete, accepts me, I accept him.

By his attitudes to me, his approach, do I know him.

I often feel it essential to completely debunk him, deflate him, humble him if he is a 'superior' type, or shows the slightest evidence of conceit or self-opinionated attitudes.

He comes to me to learn. Not I to him to teach. It is because of these attitudes that I accepted John Landy, who at nineteen years had a mile no better than 4:37, and rejected another lad who had as good a mile time at sixteen as Landy had at nineteen and who went on to run a world junior mile record at eighteen years.

Yet Landy went on to a world record of 3:57.9 and the rejected athlete has failed so far even to improve upon his eighteen-year-old best. In the case of Landy, after an unpromising start he accepted me.

These decisions, as always, were perfectly correct in both instances. No man ever makes a decision disadvantageous to himself; although others are only too ready to claim that he does. Indeed, no man is capable, in his very nature, of being untrue to himself; and that goes for the saviour as the murderer, the successful athlete as the unsuccessful.

We are all the end point, at any given moment, of our own self-expression and intrinsic worth. We just cannot add or take away from that at any instant of our being. We can proceed to enhance both our self-expression and intrinsic worth as we proceed through life – or we can fail to do so.

The future can only be a projection of ourselves and our worth. These are absolutes. All of us must abide by them – although some may be able to fool others for a time. But even these people, athletes or coaches, cannot fool everyone all the time.

So the athlete becomes part of my set-up, or he does not. The matter decides itself. If he accepts me and I accept him, he is accepted fully, at least on my part. I soon detect if he has reservations on his. If they are serious ones, we part. But this rarely occurs until he has reached the heights of his innate gifts and limitations prescribed for him. Each has his inherent limitation. These can best be seen in retrospect.

So for the present the athlete with me is fully accepted. Until proved otherwise – 'All things are possible'. He has the benefit of the doubt as to his capabilities. All my geese tend to be swans in the beginning. It is no lack in me that prescribes their development growth. That is the result of their earlier environment (teachings, etc.) and hereditary factors – both very powerful, before they come to me.

But since all is relative, I claim I work miracles upon many. It is just as meritorious to double the strength of a lad in six months as make a near-champion a champion. It is as meritorious to bring a poor type down in a season from 4:50 for the mile to 4:30 for the mile, as move the champion from 4:17 to 4:10, or an Elliott from 4:20 to 4:04 at eighteen years and a fortnight later to 4:00 4 for the mile.

I do not seek champions. I cleave to 'triers' who are sincere. The 'lesser' trying to become 'more' appeals to me more than the 'arrived' wishing to go further.

So, having survived my rudeness, directness and repellent approach, which I call a realistic approach and not a gratuitously made one, the athlete and I get together.

He comes into my home as a son. He is completely received and accepted.

His training is commenced by many hours of explanation as to the nature of things.

He is sent away to run – and keep on running. He is shown how he should run when he is strong enough to do so. He is introduced to the barbell, the sandhill, the wintry beach, the snow and the mountain height. He is expected to make himself strong, to become a man, self-reliant, assertive and convincing amongst his fellows. 'Deeds' are his argument – not words, claims, hopes, estates or 'privileges'.

Rich or poor, educated or not educated, he does the same chores, sleeps and eats as does everyone else. We are not impressed by his antecedents or personal history. If these are high, more is expected of him, that is all.

Here we are graded according to our intrinsic worth. No one can hope to be graded higher than the teacher and remain in the camp. When that day arrives, as it inevitably must, that athlete moves out, or on, and makes room for the new generation.

It is an endless process, invites no loyalties, demands no rewards and is a man-to-man competitive state that admits of no artificialities, honours, esteems, other than those most hardly won by the most painful exertions. If one fails another immediately steps in to claim the laurel wreath. I find no lack

of claimants or lads prepared to strive to their utmost. I do not need to exhort them.

So, having received the elements of the naturalistic technique, they go away and run. It is explained how this conditioning will be done, the fast and slow parts, the use of hills and sand, how they can measure their effort – what the champions before them have done – in a word 'the road' and 'the way' to excel. Some to set world records, others to attain to championship standards, some merely to improve from utter obscurity in their club or school to perhaps setting records in this field.

I can recall two lads. One an ugly duckling, weakly and gangling – he started at twenty years of age in the lower 10 per cent of the athletes in this country. He was a 'joke' in his club, rated so low as to not even making club teams. He came to me for lessons. He improved his four mile time by two minutes in one season. Awkward and uncoordinated as any athlete in my experience, he was endowed with such a simplicity of outlook, such a capacity for punishment and effort, that my heart has bled inwardly for this man. He went on to become the champion of his club in every event from the 880 to ten miles, and from memory I should include the 440.

No other athlete is ranked higher in my esteem or affection. But the world has never heard of him. His name was Les Fricker.

In our camp, Fricker is a standard – to strive like Fricker is to be ranked with the highest; as a trier and punisher he has no superior. A simple name, unhonoured and unsung elsewhere, he rates with the highest at Portsea.

Another lad who became a leading walker in this State of Victoria, realizing that walking as an event rarely attracts or demands the exertions and qualities of the distance runner, set about acquitting himself as a runner.

At twenty-one years his best time for the mile run was in the order of 4:50. In one season he moved down to sub 4:30 for the mile and went on to become, in his club, not only the walking champion over all competitive distances, but the running champion, from the 880 yards up. He, too, could claim a big success, since the success that gives me the greatest personal satisfaction is relative to beginnings, and abilities and endowments.

It is the 'overcoming', not the 'success of', that is important.

John Landy

This early action shot shows several things.

Firstly: Landy had a good running alignment, reaching out for the track without the slightest suspicion of over-striding, and showed a relaxed leg carriage and footfall.

However, his 'pacer' action, the over emphasis of his powerful thigh muscles, led to insufficient use of the arms. This in turn militated against a full sprint action in finishing and a certain amount of shoulder sway. Landy was the victim of his age. That means, born later, he could have been expected to run much faster, as could be said of all champions.

Murray Halberg, New Zealand

Best mile time: 3:57.5. Best three-mile time: 13:15. Holder world-record four mile. Winner Empire Games three mile, 1958. Virtually a one-arm runner, since an accident when a youth left this grand athlete with an all but completely useless left arm. Despite this handicap Murray Halberg has run some of the world's fastest times ever, over the one mile, two mile, three mile and up. To those who say, then, 'This proves the arms are not important,' I reply: 'Had Murray Halberg the use of two strong, effective arms, he might well have proved the greatest distance runner the world has known.'

Herb Elliott

Elliott strengthens with barbell. Note the well-developed pectoral (chest) muscles which are now considered a prime factor in fast running. Elliott, like all Portsea athletes, lifts his body-weight overhead. The three athletes in the picture with Elliott – Keenan, Bevan and Beck – all lift very heavy weights. None are muscle-bound; all very nimble and light-footed and run better than average by far, irrespective of beginnings. Personality characteristics are the usual factors that prevent athletic achievements of the highest order when they fail to be realized.

Leslie Perry

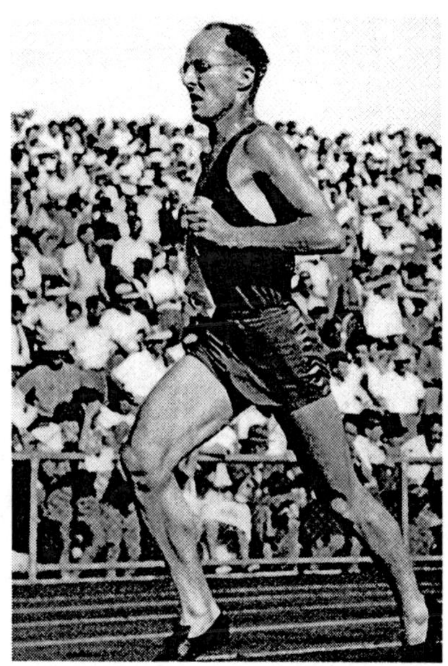

One of the first of my Australian 'Greats' who was to run a new series of Australian records from the two mile up, who proved, in his day, to be the best Olympic Games distance performer to leave Australia. Note the Nurmi-like posture and good body alignment. Perry was a hand-closed runner but certain rigidities in the chest-box area interfered with his breathing.

At Portsea, Perry is remember with honour and respect. Truly one of Australia's 'Greats'.

Betty Cuthbert

Betty Cuthbert, triple Gold Medal winner at the Olympic Games, Melbourne. Not by any means a strong muscular type, proved to be the outstanding woman speedster of her era. Her technique was completely natural, and as completely uninhibited. She ran with abandon, every muscle doing its part, 'including the facials', as I have taught for years. Many a male athlete, stultified in his poker-faced, stereotyped movements, could do well to study the technique as so perfectly demonstrated by the young lady.

Miss Cuthbert ran with the 'brakes' completely 'off', and did not need any dubious masculine characteristics of leanness, size or muscularity to prove her fleetness of foot. I would say that Miss Cuthbert evinced all the many points of perfection of style and effectiveness, with grace and beauty, that I have preached about for years.

CHAPTER 4

Ray Weinberg

The fastest Australian hurdler ever, Weinberg improved his 120 yard (110 metres) hurdle time by .3 sec., after experimenting with his hurdling techniques, to become the third fastest in the world of that year. Weinberg, with a fastest 100 yards of only 9.9 seconds, was set against the faster sprint times of the best American-trained hurdlers. His real claim to fame is not his Australian record of 14 dead, which still stands, nor his sixth in the 1952 Games, when on times he could have been expected to run third, but the fact that his 'differential' was proved to be the best in the world. This means that Weinberg had mastered the art of getting back to the track, after taking-off, faster than any other hurdler; of being airborne for a less time. Had Australia the sprinters fast enough it could be that we could produce hurdlers as we appear to produce milers. My personal testimony is that Weinberg, as a man, was even greater than as an athlete. Esteemed by all, Ray was captain of the athletic team in the Olympic Games, 1952.

CHAPTER 5

An appreciation that the 'power rests within us', and great performances in life are produced outside the realm of the fortuitous and the adventitious – great performance is the result of the intrinsic worth as found and developed in the individual.

It resides outside of the fact of race, colour, creed and, to some extent, opportunity – great athletes rise and create their destiny. For them life seems to be moulded to their pattern, rather than they are moulded by life – always the great athlete creates the schedule – never does the schedule create the great athlete

The great, truly great, athlete will early realize his destiny, his role, his power of accomplishment. He will sense this rather than know it, so a certain degree of wonderment at his own performances will be mixed with his feelings of predestination and certainty.

For him, he will find, there is no alternative – only changes of direction. The die is cast: he accepts his lot – the work, the ends and goals.

He is indifferent to persuasions and threats. He will carve his own life. When he fails to achieve the highest, the fault or defect lie in him. It was always there. He also realized it and will not be altogether grief-stricken or completely dismayed at his failure.

What is this power within us?

Some call it God. Bergson called it the *élan vital.* Bluntly, I see it as the life principle and its measure is in the degree of the intensity in which it is found in us. We have it, or we do not have it, to a degree ever-varying from individual to individual, no two *exactly* to the same quality or quantity.

It is evidenced by great natural powers of endurance or power to survive: the body, in the beginning, may be weakly, but the spirit will be strong. The will to survive will be strong: the intellect will be powerful and instinctively know much that makes for survival. There will be an intense enthusiasm for life – a zest for living, a dissatisfaction with the *status quo*, a wonderment, interest and identification with all things human and natural. The appetite for know-how will be unquenchable.

All this is linked up with this universal spirit of which we find ourselves a powerful or dominating vehicle. Or we don't: and we can do little about it, either way, really.

In athletes this spirit will find its outlet in competition and achievement. Commencing with what 'capital' we possess, we nevertheless press on. The 'impossible' is reasonable to these people. Never entirely daunted: resilient: thoughtful – determination to succeed, somehow, somewhere and in some things, seems to be a normal part of their make-up.

Patience and courage, the ability to wait, to try and to suffer, is taken for granted.

Such an athlete is a seeker above all. He burns to know. He will believe 'all things are possible' – it is not having the 'know-how' that *temporarily* holds him up. He goes about seeking it.

He may not talk about it, but he will be of those who believe 'Ask, and it is given us' (as we are able to assimilate and digest, by growth) – 'Seek, and we do find' – even if the 'way' be long – very long: tough – very tough: painful and discouraging – we never give up hope – entirely, and that, when we 'knock,' sincerely, honestly, humbly, doors of knowledge and help do open to us, remarkable and 'lucky' as it appears to others.

The rewards of sincere effort are exactly proportionate to the 'powers within us'. The power is added to by effort and experience, until in the end, as Nurmi and Zatopek proved, the impossible becomes reasonable, the abnormal our norm, when we are compared with our fellows.

No door remains for ever locked against the man of indomitable will and courage. What we most lack is the power to continue: continuity and perseverance – the never-quit spirit *allied to intelligence* is the secret key to success: *not* great natural endowments, powerful friends and favourable environments such as the great Physical Culture Centre, or the wealthy university. These things can be aids. They can as easily become unwelcome props removing primitive struggle from the essential path of the tyro.

In high endeavour nothing can be conferred, nothing can be 'willed' to another: All must be 'earned'. There is no royal road to the top. It only 'appears' to be so.

For any *worthwhile* achievement highly valued by knowledgeable men, sweat and tears, often blood, is the normal concomitant.

Nothing easily attained was ever worth while: nothing worth while easily attained to. This is the law.

In this world, all, in the final analysis, is law, or the result of law. There is no 'chance' – it only 'appears' to be so.

Indeed powerful personalities always make their own chances opportunities and always did, and always will, impose their will upon their weaker brethren.

The dead know nothing of these things. To die prematurely, to quit halfway up the mountain, is merely evidence, as I view it, of a limited intelligence – no matter how academically high that intelligence appears to be – and a weakly endowment of life spirit. No man can be blamed for his endowments or lack of them. In utter truth he cannot even be blamed for his failings and inabilities to continue along his chosen path. But he can be known, judged and appraised by his reactions to life, his progress and *attained* goals.

What he may not realize is – if he is one destined to proceed – never to entirely quit – the strength – the power, *is added as we need it* – since it is a quality of absolute illimitability: since it is all. In a word, no man failed because of a shortage of the God – Stuff – or Spirit. It is that he was a poor vessel or vehicle, that is all.

In the end *all* cancel out equal. Those destined to great aims and ends are crucified in the process, those not so destined find life fair and easy. Truly do we all have our rewards. Just as truly we are what we are.

But! No man knows what he may become, although he will suspect his abilities or his lacks. It is not until the last page of the last chapter is written can he, or any man, say with certainty how much he has succeeded, or by how much he has failed. *That* is the prerogative of posterity.

This much is true: we can become as great an athlete as we reasonably conceive of ourselves and hold the view honestly and continuously.

Hopes and wishful thinkings soon collapse and disappear. The power to do remains with us, if it is in us. It may change direction, may change its form, but it never entirely deserts us or leaves us, even if we think it has gone at times.

It is for us to develop our full powers as we can. It is for the way-pointer, the coach, to indicate the road. Every athlete must do his own conditioning and training: welcome and accept his own suffering and pains. There is no other way.

As a coach, I am but an elder brother – a way-shower – one who has travelled the way and would help, encourage, sustain and cheer on the fellow travellers, who stumble, often blindly, up the heights to fulfilment.

But there is little commiseration, little in the way of sympathy or the shedding of mutual tears, no grieving over our sores or wounds.

The elder must always stand up and watch the process of

learning and suffering. His heart may bleed within him for what he sees and feels, but few or no words can ever pass his lips.

No man ever climbed on weakly sentimentality, sympathy or excuses. True men will suffer alone and resent intrusions in their darkest hours, indifferent to all others, and they temporarily remain submerged in their own torments and agonies of spirit. They never invite sympathy, nor do they need it.

'Tis thus we know them – the athletes and the coaches: the weakly and the strong ones.

Whilst there is life there can be progress. Athletically we must pass the zenith of our times and distances some day, it is true. But the character and personality arising from our activities will not decrease as we descend the arc of physical prowess. Indeed, it will be added to in order that we, in our turn, can be 'towers of strength' to the next generation – encouraging, expounding, urging and goading.

Success *can* be certain.

Those who feel great powers within them *have* great powers within them, even if they cannot immediately demonstrate what they would wish, or yearn, to demonstrate.

The serious athlete does well to remember there is no haste on the creative plane, that Nature cannot be hurried, that the greater the eventual accomplishment, the longer the time, the more strenuous the effort.

For to those who have – much is added. To those who have not – they soon lose even what prowess or powers they may have started out with. No tears are shed. Nor need be.

The man who sheds tears, real or figuratively, because of his own sufferings or chagrin, is not a man, but a woman.

Real men are known by their attitudes, as well as their deeds. They neither fawn upon their betters nor expect or demand considerations other than those conceded to their equals.

In this they will be found to fight for their rights – whatever they may be deemed to be.

Therefore, they will fight for what they want, where they want to go – and not expect 'lifts' or concessions. They will view their fellow competitors with suspicion until they discover they can honestly respect them. Until then they will be reserved, even lack cordiality.

An over-abundant cordiality, anxiety to please, subservience or uncritical respect for authority was never a characteristic of the great athlete or the great man, in any field or activity. Wealth or 'honours' were never a true measure of greatness nor manliness, although they can be.

Athletes destined for high endeavour will feel too strongly their own powers within themselves to accord too much to others.

It is only the weak who look up to the strong: the strong are usually too busy, pushing down the weakly, to look up to anyone!

To be self-contained: not to need the flatteries and adulations so commonly bestowed: indeed, to feel a secret contempt for the bestowers is a concomitant of greatness, wherever it is found.

Much is tolerated, sometimes resented, by those who have greatness thrust upon them. If they luxuriate in these states and honours, they fail by just that much to achieve true greatness.

Truly by their 'acts' do we know them.

Hogan and Agostini

Hec Hogan (Australia) and Mike Agostini (Trinidad). The picture shows the poor running styles and movements adopted by two of the world's greatest sprinters when running under extreme stress. Hogan is looking skywards whilst Agostini has turned slightly sideways. It may well be argued that either one is right and the other wrong., if we are to view such positions from the criteria of perfection. The far-flung arm positions of both sprinters are wasteful of energy and tend to unbalance the runner. It is in attention to such details, so neglected as most pictures of athletes indicate, that we can expect the faster times of the 'dash' runners to come.

In many cases the fast men have not been conditioned to add strength or agility. These two factors might easily cause the balance of supremacy to pass to the country that seriously bothers to study and develop such details of technique.

Two one mile world record juniors – Elliott and Clarke

This is an interesting study in slight variations. Clarke had run a world junior mile record of 4:6.8, to lose it to Elliott, who ran 4:6 and later 4:4.4, whilst still under nineteen years.

Elliott already shows more determination in face and fist, and carries his head in better alignment than does Ron, who tends to 'come up'.

Both have the low arm carriage. Elliott's more powerful pectorals can be seen through his vest. Note the free full stride and the foot about to make contact. No attempt is being made at all to control the landing, much less a 'ball of foot' landing.

Ron had his first lesson in running from me at the Caulfield Racecourse in the days when I conducted Sunday morning classes there. He was then seventeen years of age. It is true that he later varied his training from the well-known Fartlek ideas then current in our State of Victoria, and seemed to adopt the interal-type training which was being popularized, doing most of his training on the track.

Chapter 6

On relaxation: too often it is the *sine qua non* for easy effort – there may be a new approach?

I hold that relaxation *per se* cannot be taught. I hold that it is a negative state and as such is the repose condition that follows the exercise of power and strength. It is the natural corollary of effort. It never can be effort itself.

It is true when we see an athlete in a state of tension and strain we say 'Relax'. It is true we find that when he ceases making an effort that is bound up in tension and strain, that is, eases up or stops trying, he seems to do better.

But the truth, as I understand it, is that the athlete should be taught how to exert his full power *without* tension or strain and that *easing the effort* is not the answer. At least it never was the answer of the weight-lifter trying to hoist some colossal weight over his head and getting stuck halfway!

Where the technique is understood – and taught – where the science and art of delivering full power without stress and strain is understood, the word relaxation is seldom used. Nor need it be. I have seen men battling up to a finishing–line, hands clenched, and have heard them being told to relax.

I have seen other athletes attempting to finish flat out with extended fingers and every sinew of the neck standing out like cords with tension – not conquering power, and strain in every lineament.

Because it so happens that such an athlete may have achieved a world record – I have in mind the Australian Shirley Strickland (later Mrs. de la Hunty) – such typical cases in no wise prove my contentions wrong.

What is proved, as I see it, is, in some fields such as women's athletics athletes can get away with attitudes and techniques not possible to top world–record performance amongst male athletes, nor especially of the male athlete, or the records, of the future.

Whilst discussing women performers – and in case the reader may imagine I see no good at all in women competitors – let me put on record that the woman athlete Betty Cuthbert, in my considered opinion, showed the best 'form' and the greatest capacity for 'outpouring' running of any athlete of the Melbourne Games, man or woman. A close scrutiny of the tight features, semi–closed mouths, inhibited and strained efforts of all other sprinters must bear out my contention. The next to Miss Cuthbert in this capacity for true relaxation combined with the delivery of *full* power must be accorded to the great distance–runner Vladimir Kuts.

Zatopek, in his day, was, of course, the greatest exponent of relaxed uninhibited punishing effort, despite what the pundits think or say. How much of his phenomenal successes in his day was due to his personal technique, no one will ever accurately evaluate. But it is significant that those who have attempted to follow his training ideas and schedules have singularly failed to achieve his results or eminence in their relation to *their* contemporaries.

To me, there can be no true relaxation *combined with full power* whilst the hands *remain* open. The opening and closing of the hands in a distance–runner can be associated with rest and drive.

But I hold that Mimoun failed by just that lack of understanding in his many tussles over the years with Zatopek.

The pictures of Zatopek finishing in the 5,000 metres at

Helsinki is evidence enough for me.

Relaxation, therefore, must be considered as the negative part of power exerted, and *not* a desirable or positive quality in itself.

To me, the only truly relaxed athlete is he who functions fully in his power and strength so that his muscle repose, or rest, state is natural and normal.

Relaxation, therefore, can never be the result of an act of will, nor can it be taught as a technique: it must be a result of: never a thing in itself. This, to me, is the cardinal error in athletics, as it is taught, and when the principle is more fully understood, so will sprint performances especially tend to improve.

I would say that athletic performances have been more retarded by the inadvisable resorting to relaxation as a 'cure–all' than by any other single fallacy in which the practice of athletes would appear to abound.

I would say that to teach a weak athlete to relax is to teach him to acquire a further set of tensions that, instead of aiding his performance, is more likely to hinder his advancement.

For an athlete to attempt to relax by direction, or will, the result will be:

1. Further tensions resulting from trying to abolish tension.
2. A weakly non–positive, non–effectual attitude that militates against high–level performance.

It is true that a mind put at rest removes tension and a musculature that instinctively responds will provide its own relaxation and the coach can help remove some of the tensions that arise from lack of confidence – another word for the one great human evil, *fear*.

The strong rest – call it relax if you will: a man fighting for his life has little time to rest or relax.

It is equally true of an athlete who over–tries: who strains to the point of loss of good form – he also will not achieve satisfactory, much less maximum, results.

But, by and large, relaxation as most generally propounded, conceived of, and taught in athletics is mostly the imaginative concept of weakly men and coaches.

It is curious that in my years of association with competing weight-lifters, and my lesser association with wrestlers and the like, the word relaxation is never used or heard.

It is also true that, as a competitor, it is easier to run relaxed in poor time, than it is to hoist double the body weight overhead – or to pin a powerful, violent wrestling opponent. It is even more futile for a fighter to attempt to deliver a knock–out punch relaxed and with a non–clenched fist.

Maybe the advocates of relaxation for the runner have never been participants in either the fight game or the iron game. I would think so.

So I reject relaxation, except as a temporary rest process that permits the full effort, whatever it may be, to continue. No man can maintain full power and pressure indefinitely. Neither can he deliver *full* power and effort with ease – or in a state of relaxation.

If the use of the word was abolished, and the word 'rest cycle' or pulse was adopted, we may, as coaches and athletes, advance the cult of athletics a little further. As I see it, the more common use of the word indicates the weaker types and for that reason is to be deplored.

Athletics – especially the events that do not require the sincere and arduous training of the four–minute miler, the twenty–eight–minute six–miler, or the sub–2:30 marathon man, for example – and the athletes associated with such other events seem to me to reverberate most often to the word relaxation. We never use it, or teach it, at Portsea, I hasten to add, *in the accepted sense.*

This is not to say I do not understand what is true relaxation and a relaxed effort. But I never ever saw or could conceive of a superlative run, jump or throw that did not require all that the athlete could pack into the effort. If such an athlete and effort is also synonymous with ease and relaxation, then the whole subject and matter is a contradiction in terms.

When we understand how to pulse, which entails the use of our natural rhythms in our efforts, relaxation becomes as normal a component – as natural and 'taken for granted' – as courage, effort and the high resolves of the class athlete.

The weakly wrist action, the shambling, shivering and prancing that so often goes for relaxation, is ludicrous as well as useless. We can 'shake out our tensions' – we can work our musculature into proper attitudes and postures – but the accepted ideas as to relaxation play no part in my scheme of, or fitness of things.

Yet it must be admitted that a totally wrong approach: the calling up of the will unduly: wrong deduction: can easily ruin what should be a world–class athletic career. I have in mind a young and strong athlete, who at eighteen years, in his first year of athletics, found himself junior 880–yard champion of his country. In the next three years he was senior 880–yard champion. He added some other championships to his list: at twenty–two years of age his career, as far as going on to world championships, appeared to be over. How did this come about?

This young athlete had discovered that work did things. When he wanted to step up the level of his performance he merely stepped up the work done in training.

Such a solution is not necessarily a true one as this athlete, in the end, admitted to me.

However, during the process of self–ruin, nothing I could do or say would convince this young man that his approach was irrational: he had to go through the personal experience and personally discover the truth for himself. Whether he has irrevocably ruined his future possibilities, no one, not even the athlete himself, can know.

It may be that his early successes were his undoing. How

simple it seemed when training for one hour a day produced a 1:54 880; then merely training for two hours a day 'must reduce my time to 1:52' reasoned this athlete. If he found that it did – it was easy to take the next step and double the training to reduce the time to a sub–1:50 880.

It does not work that way. Such a solution is far too obvious, too simple, to be true.

In this young man's case, he ended up with training sessions, doggedly persisted with, of around twenty miles a day. The result was *slower* than ever 880's, and the ability to run the marathon – and then, not in world–class time.

No athlete in my experience ever indicated more clearly the futility of the simple adage 'Work does things' – then, to do better, double the work, treble the work, quadruple the work. It is all too fatuous.

Work *does* do things. But work *simple* never did great things or every labourer would become a rich man. Every one who trained sincerely and long – a champion. We know they do not.

It is the quality of the work that is important. Let us quote our adage again: Work does things. *Intelligent* work does things better.

We must for ever be calling up our intelligence factor as we proceed towards our pre–determined goals.

It is because coaches observe athletes who over–try, over–train, who tie–up with an unintelligent approach and determination, that the cry has gone up – 'Relax'.

Indeed, I could quote other cases. One Australian, now in the U.S.A., made himself; probably, the physically strongest sprinter in the world – but he still did not run fast.

Power, wrongly exerted, can actually stop us, bring us to a standstill. The defect, or disease, is one of the mentality. I have known three cases in my personal experience, all of them junior champions, who have failed to fulfil their early promise simply because they believed that more and more determined and conscientious effort was the sole solution and the royal road to world–class success as a senior athlete.

Such is this attitude a 'disease of the mind', that the cure does not appear to rest in a slackening off of the effort, nor even in a cessation from training altogether.

The mind, drilled and grilled to wrong concepts, reacts against itself. The result is that as the athlete tries hard, the power exerted is transferred to his antagonistic muscles and the harder he exerts his power (mental, determination, etc.) – the harder he tries – the more his *brakes pull on*.

Such an athlete will run until he is shockingly distressed and will have the chagrin of finding himself passed in the latter stages of a race and find that there is no power or solution that he can call upon to end his unenviable plight.

I feel that the cause of all this lies in the early athletic education – or lack of it.

The inherent intelligence of the athlete has not been great enough, unaided, to guide him rightfully to his ends and solutions.

His reasoning faculties seized upon the too obvious what, may be called the superficial, and accepted it as truth.

The only 'cure' that I know of is a slow re–education. A going–back, if it is possible and a re–starting, all over again.

The athlete who has lost the ability to relax normally can be re–educated. He can be taken back along his bitter road of disappointment and punishing effort, until he reaches a place where he does not need to exert himself to do a thing with the customary over–use of his will.

His physical movements need to be re–organized. Indeed, mentally and physically, it is a case of re–education. I have, myself; never had a completely successful outcome. I am in process of attempting a 'cure' on a young Englishman.

Capable at nineteen years of age of a 4:13 mile – at twenty–one years, although bigger and stronger, he is incapable of running a mile in that time.

It is evident that the strength and power is there to run a four–minute mile. The sacrifices made and the training endured have been sufficient to make a three–minute mile a reality – to take the matter to the absurd.

Surely this problem must be the most serious that a coach, and an athlete, ever has to encounter and resolve.

But the cry of 'Relax' is also too simple a remedy. How to relax and yet deliver full power is not as easy as it appears, on the surface.

I would go so far as to say the problems and associated psychological states are beyond the scope of the ordinary coach, except he be trained in some manner in psychology.

I would repeat, merely to tell the athlete to relax – even show him *how* to relax – is no solution in really bad cases.

I would suggest that the athlete be taken out of regular training, his mind diverted to other absorbing interests, or studies, even sports, such as mountain walking and swimming.

Swimming is particularly good, since in no other sport, unless it be golf; is it so evident that great power, wrongly exerted, results in poorer and yet poorer effort. The swimmer who determines to pull himself through the water by sheer exertion of strength soon learns two things. He merely 'pulls holes in the water' and soon comes to a standstill – or should it be 'float–still'? – from physical exhaustion. There is an art and skill in exerting power to the best advantage in swimming. Unless this is understood and acquired, no one becomes a really great and fast swimmer.

The same principles apply in running and other athletic pursuits.

Power *must* be there. Nothing can be done today without great strength – mostly developed and in–built, since we are now functioning above the results derived from natural strength as found in the *endowed* athlete.

The champion today needs added strength, built–in by added exercise – but the acquiring of this added strength appears to be fraught with much danger.

The athlete can easily become tied–up (possibly out of this arose the old cry 'muscle–bound'). It is the coach's job, above all else, to steer the athlete through the shoals and shallow reasonings that often end in futility and wrongly directed power output.

Yet the solution is not in the conscious mind of the unfortunate athlete so afflicted. His unconscious must be reached. Reasoning with him is useless. He listens, even agrees, but appears to be unable to act. His old habit patterns, derived often from years of wrong application, are too powerful.

His solution, I can but repeat, is to take the 'patient' back to his early beginnings, and slowly, gradually, bring him back along the road to class performance and success. This needs constant and strict supervision.

All attempts to race fast must be abandoned. Indeed, it is better if the athlete completely abandons all competition for the season in which the 'cure' is operating.

An athlete should be 're–made' in a year. If this cannot be done *in that time, he is better* advised to move to another sport, one that makes less demands upon concentration and competition: mountain walking is one such pastime. Distance swimming could be another, or long–distance running, even.

The handling of really heavy weights, also, soon breaks down the psychological condition, as long as the athlete ceases to apply his will and merely lifts with his strength. It is the weight-lifter who understands the niceties of applying full power and the danger of the continual over–use of the will.

The actual balance must ever be a very delicate one.

The athlete who is nicely balanced or adjusted in this regard, strength for strength, will excel over his less finely balanced brother athlete.

This is a matter of temperament, probably an inherited factor, more than a developed or educated one. Fortunate indeed is the athlete singularly endowed in this respect.

But the actual existence of this balance appears to be wrapped up in the condition I speak of as 'high intelligence'. The matter is instinctive: the solution self–evident: the results – certain, despite the pitfalls and occasional stumblings on the upward path to great performance.

Hence, I feel and repeat, the great, truly great, athlete is born with his capabilities: his ultimates are pre–determined for him – all he has to do is to faithfully 'travel the way'. Whether he does so or not depends, in the final analysis, upon his 'character'. This latter is also largely an inherent factor: rather, the *temperament* that results in character is innate, the ethics and moralities upon which character is founded – these are the result of education, and experience is a vital part of education.

So we find that to be exhorted to relax is not as easy a solution as it may at first appear, and the means to relax is not necessarily obtained by dangling forearms and sagging jaws – both more appropriate to the idiot than the world–class athlete. No, sir, true relaxation is not so simple as that!

Chapter 7

Success in athletics is the result, primarily, of certain states, intermixed as variables. These are: (1) High intelligence (2) Inborn intrinsic worth (3) Natural gifts (4) High–level tuition

Definitely, I make marked distinctions in my appraisal of intelligence and intelligent people. Even more definitely am I not impressed because some authority studied here, or studied there: Academic degrees are mostly merely tickets to practise something. When they have anything to do with physical fitness, athletics and the like, they are suspect with me.

It is true many academicians *were* highly intelligent. The works of the best of them stand upon my book–shelves. We mast rank Einstein amongst the highest of the moderns. The world of books teems with great names from Plato and Jesus to Leonardo da Vinci and Michelangelo to Carrell and Freud. (Freud being notably rejected in his own time.)

But to imagine that education confers 'high' intelligence is, to me, to put one amongst the foolish. It *can* confer degrees of high intelligence, but does not necessarily do so. I start from there. Indeed, I will go so far as to say that there is not one more highly intelligent person in the world, at any time, because of education. The highly intelligent always did – and always will – educate themselves. The means to do so come easy to them.

As Kant, I think it was, said: in teaching, he never bothered about the dull ones – they were too stupid, anyway. And the clever ones, they found out for themselves and did not need teaching. So he bothered to teach only the middle group – the mediocre ones. I find that mostly true in the teaching of athletes.

How can we determine who is highly intelligent in the athletic sense – and how do we rate them? In what way will they differ from their fellows?

Firstly, they will know much, even before they have been taught – and mostly will differ, even if in silence, with their early coaches and teachers.

They will be quick to learn anything new, and will remain silent during lectures, except to ask a pertinent question. They will never ask a foolish question. Their questions will show a complete grasp of the subject being taught, and will tend to carry the subject matter further. They will have far above average powers of deduction. They will never need to be told important things twice. In a word they will not only be good pupils – they will gain the admiration of the teacher who quickly recognizes their inherent abilities.

Such athletes will be restless with poor teachers and immediately recognize the impostor: the mountebank: the charlatan.

The highly intelligent are never 'yes, sir' men. They reflect, and agree – or they do not.

It is not always the most highly intelligent who get marked highest in academic examinations. Often their work is above the examiner who may (1) resent, consciously or unconsciously, – the obvious superiority, or (2) may not understand the merit of the paper and mark it down because it did not fit in with his idea of what constituted the correct or perfect answer.

Generally speaking, unless the lecturer and examiner is singularly gifted, I would say that to have a very high intelligence can handicap one academically in the pursuit of honours and degrees which tend to fall to the more orthodox clever. After all, much 'learning' is memory.

Knowledge need not necessarily be either.

High intelligence provides a truer attitude to life as to basic, real or natural essentials, called phenomena. A man of high intelligence may have to conform – but he will know when and how he is conforming and will never mistake the truth for the spurious, the real for the unreal.

When high intelligence is at work we will cease to try and 'work it out' to plan. He will 'feel' and *know* how it will work out.

Indeed, I view with the greatest suspicion the results derived from the intellectual processes of reason and working it out by conscious thought (thinking about it).

In my experience, to find the truth as to any personal decision that has to be made, or arrived at, one acquires as much of the relevant data as the case, or position, demands by its importance, urgency, etc., and then abandons all conscious thought until a decision finally becomes permanent in the being. We then know and that decision will always be right for us. When we consciously review the pros and cons, try to thrash it out consciously, we mostly, it seems to me, arrive at decisions dubious as to truth and reality, even for ourselves.

A typical case is when we try to determine by intellectual processes our attitudes to another – as to respect, regard, affection or duty. We may determine these things, especially as to the last, duty, but if our attitudes are not based in 'truth in feeling' we soon become restless under our assumed burdens, duties, whatever they may be.

So the athlete is taught, if he can be – it is mostly instinctive, – to rely upon himself and his day–to–day and lap–to–lap feelings and impressions, as they well up into consciousness.

The athlete is taught to act in this way, and to rely upon it, both as to training and to racing.

In both he will have a general or overall plan, but he will be quick to amend his plan as the fitness of the moment appears to demand.

To function successfully in this way, there must be a more

or less fearless approach – neither a lack of confidence nor an over–confidence and a habit of serious evaluation of all the other competitors. No man, or athlete, can know without prior experience, or some historical background, as to the race or the athletes in it. So he is advised to keep well in touch with all that he may hear or see concerning his opponents, the nature of the track, and the like. He will test all information that comes to him by his experience, and take nothing for granted. If it does not seem right or true he will reject, or further check–up.

Nothing is too unimportant to interest a man of high intelligence, and he will soon learn to judge immediately and instinctively as to his informants and their veracity.

The matter of intrinsic worth. How does that differ from high intelligence? In this way: a man might easily have a very high intelligence and use it, say, as did Einstein and Rutherford use theirs.

But such a man may have a very gentle or sensitive nature: recoil, for instance, from the 'violent' approach. Prefer to let preferments go rather than fight for them, or over them. His intrinsic worth will be of a different order to another, whose high intelligence equals that of our scientists, but whose combative nature fits him more readily for his role as a great statesman, nation builder or athlete.

His intrinsic worth is, then, of a different order, but not necessarily less because of his vocation, or life work.

In this world there is room, and need, for all types and conditions.

We can measure high intelligence readily enough, but intrinsic worth is a much more variable and indefinite part of personality, at least in my view. The intrinsic worth of the great athlete will readily show out, not only in a highly intelligent approach to his athleticism, but in great courage: a marked dominating attitude: a resistance to the fatigues, both physical and mental, that tend to break down others. He will not only be intelligent, but he will be 'big' amongst his fellows – in personality, leadership and those characteristics that mark him out as a man amongst men. He affects to be nothing: he merely is.

Natural gifts: I hold we *all* have one, or more, for something. Even the least and meanest of us.

Because our natural gifts may not be in art, music or commerce, folk are inclined to depreciate the gifts, even deplore them, unless they fit in with urban life and our vaunted civilization.

Take the gift of running, as an example, or the gift of great strength, that enables us to be a champion weight-lifter, eventually. Both are looked upon as inferior to the gift of memory, or a talent for mathematics, or buying and selling, or finance. Yet in war–time, on holidays, even around the workshop or home, the gift of agility and strength may save the gifted one's life – or the life of another.

In primitive emergency our gifts are put to their real tests. A financial brain but poor swimming ability is a poor standby in a shipwreck or a boating disaster.

My advice to all is – seek out your gift – you will be sure to have one, and develop it assiduously for its own sake. A man named Larry Adler did just this with the common mouth–organ. He has raised that humble musical instrument to the rank of harmonica and the playing of it to an art that may well rank with any top–line musician of the day.

Despise nothing, for who knows the gift of suppleness may be all that is needed to make one a great pole–vaulter, since strength is much more easily acquired than an inordinate sense of balance and suppleness.

And so we could continue *ad infinitum*. Therefore seek out your gift or gifts. If it appears to be in athletics, in running for example, develop it and exploit it. Every man derives great satisfaction in doing only one thing, maybe, well. And once he starts in on the job of developing and exploiting his gift, even if it appear not to be too wonderful in the beginning, be assured that practice, patience and pertinacity – the three 'P's – can work miracles. In all these matters – time is the factor.

It may take one athlete four months to move from 4:10 for the mile to four minutes. It may take another four years. What of it? The view from any mountain top above 20,000 feet is much the same from century to century.

Indeed, in this regard, there are often many paths, or routes, to any objective – and each man will find his a little different to each and every other man.

Hence the fallacy, or falsity, of the fixed schedule: the mileage per day, or the speeds and rests of the efforts.

Elliott reached 4:00.4 for the mile from 4:20, with probably one–tenth – possibly one–twentieth – of the training and mileage that John Landy took to move from 4:09 to 4:02 for the mile. What of it? What is important is that *both* excel: that *both* run world records. The age it is done: the place: the track: the training mileages: the schedules – are these so important?

I strongly hold that if embryo champions spent more time discovering and developing themselves, and less time endeavouring to find out the minute details of some new champion or world record–breaker's schedule . . .!

It is the *principles* of training and conditioning that are important. The detailed schedules are of interest only and never can be considered dogmatic, even generally applicable to others.

There are certain common denominators, it is true, certain minimums of time and effort, I feel, at least. But what they are, and to whom they will apply, it is a wise coach indeed, unless he has a very intimate relationship over a long period, who can dogmatize even in a general way to his athletes.

I teach them to learn to know themselves: test and try out for themselves. Find what they can tolerate and what they cannot. To experiment ceaselessly.

I but suggest the means and point the 'way'. I watch and suggest: I find I have mostly to suggest less work rather than exhort to more. One young athlete, only twenty–one years as I write this, never even conceived it within the bounds of his human possibility that he might run in the Olympic Games in Melbourne. He finished fifth in the 5,000 metres incidentally. I found it necessary, in his year's preparation for the Games, to cut his own self–devised training regime by fifty per cent. He immediately started to improve. This was done about six months before the Games.

So the coach finds the *good* ones tend to be *over*–meticulous, over–conscientious, too consistent, and his main job is to watch for evidence of strain, over–doing it and breakdown.

In time the athlete himself will be able to fairly accurately evaluate his own needs, strengths and possibilities, even from day to day. This is how it should be: The coach, then, merely becomes a 'back–stop', a 'good friend', and, perhaps, a 'learner' from what he sees and hears. No one can listen and look who talks *all* the time is an axiom many coaches would do well to remember.

Lastly, I list high–level tuition, and ask where is it to be found? *That* is a question many an athlete would like to know the answer to. Some travel from one country to another in the search, only to find an athlete of his new country has departed to where he has just left!

There are many good coaches, I have no doubt at all, and widely diversified. Good coaches, like good athletes, seem to be thrown up anywhere, at any time, and to – as irresponsibly (it would appear) – subside and disappear.

But this can be taken as axiomatic. One good athlete may be thrown up, and develop himself, but if there is a continuity, a sequence, there is a good coach or mentor hidden somewhere close by, even if his name is not mentioned in the annals of fame.

And if we go to that place, we will find that he is well known enough to the discerning, although these may be few in numbers.

Publicity, notoriety, these can be based in works or words. But if the coach is not worthy, in time one can observe a small but steady stream setting in, in an *opposite* direction.

There is a kind of freemasonry amongst good athletes: the word soon gets around and in time a first–class coach – wherever he may be located – will find athletes will travel to him. Such a coach does not need to advertise, to publicize; his athletes and their feats speak for him. There just is no other measure of value in athletics, anyhow. As a coach myself I am at a loss how to evaluate what is high–level tuition without making myself my own model. Modesty, false or real, in our civilization deems this impossible.

But high–level tuition, obviously, can only exude from a high–level coach, and I cannot imagine either without some claims somewhere to high–level performance. Not that to be able to perform well means one is a natural teacher. That, also, is an innate gift in its highest expression. But he will be a *demonstrable* master of his subject, our high–level coach. He may no longer be able to clear six feet in the high–jump, but if he is good he will always *look* like a champion, even if only clearing three feet six inches, and will show an agility, poise and performance that must mark him out above his fellows.

High–level coaches do not teach *from* books: they teach from knowledge and experience which may, or may not, be confirmed in books by other coaches. He who, perforce, must rely upon what another has said must always be something less than he who relies upon something he has personally experienced.

No illiterate man could possibly be a high-level coach in these days of science and higher education. Indeed, the high-level coach today, it seems to me, must need be a symposium of all the sciences – at least in some degree, and *really* knowledgeable in quite a few. To achieve this takes time, study and experience. He is not likely to be in his teens, or in his twenties, by my standards. He could be at his best when seventy or eighty even.

There is no limit to experience, wisdom and knowledge. But there is when the years are few. May the good coaches' years be long upon the Earth, says the prophet!

CHAPTER 7

Charles (Chilla) Porter

The greatest high jumper produced by Australia. Limited in opportunities to study techniques out of Australia, and limited in opportunities to get incentive from competition, Australian high jumpers have ever been a very small band of enthusiasts, separated, often, by thousands of miles. Nevertheless Winter won at the London [Olympics], and Porter gained second place in the Melbourne Olympics. Porter developed his technique with the aid of his coach in Queensland, a State unable to provide a jumping venue of first class standard.

Porter, determined to go further, if possible, is another young athlete willing to come over one thousand miles from home to work and live in Victoria, in order to obtain the benefit of the better jumping conditions and study first hand our conditioning methods.

Ray Smith

Ray Smith walked sixth in the fifty kilometre event at the 1956 Olympic Games, won by Norm Reed.

A regular visitor for training at Portsea, this walker, noted for his good and fair style, often trained with the runners. Conversant with our techniques, as was Reed, Smith also applied them successfully.

The picture shows the absolute fairness of his heel and toe technique. Much of Smith's stamina training was done in walking on the road from Melbourne to Portsea, the total distance of which is sixty miles.

Herb Elliott

Elliott running alone in the race which gave him the Australian 3,000 metres and three mile junior records, the last that he was to take from Ron Clarke, and to complete his series.

Although not yet nineteen years of age, he shows the typical Elliott running style and determined approach that was to make him the most famous mile runner ever in the history of athletics.

Chapter 8

In conclusion, and to repeat, the belief, adamant in my teachings, is that the athlete must be developed in the end, so that he be entirely self–reliant, self–dependent, able to know instinctively and understand his nature, personality trends, and his requirements in exercise and training, from day to day, month to month.

That he instinctively, by inner divination, senses his strength and ability and the ebb and flow of both – That he feels a responsibility, in the end, only to himself as a unique organism even if it be within the corporate body or state – In this way only, I opine, can the athlete ever come face to face with himself as an athlete and a man: to be indifferent alike to praise or censure, honours or defeats, and to realize he is what he is, and does – because he is. He needs no other incentives, duties, loyalties – such an athlete, and man, who I adjudge is the ultimate, will be positive in outlook, dominating as to his environment, successful in his attempted achievements – at least, mostly

I attempt to teach these aspects, and in this order:

1. To be a man, functionally complete and efficient.
2. To be a 'leader' in his chosen environment, society, field of activity, occupation or profession.

3. That to be successful as an athlete is one of the disciplines that should lead to the other two.

No door is closed to the advancing personality, whether in athletics or any other sphere of activity.

It is my aim to break down two widespread convictions that, perhaps, hamper youth in their development more than any other two such single concepts.

The first alleges that one needs to be born singularly gifted, in some privileged – or 'lucky' sense. Let it be said that in Nature there are no 'privileged' persons: they only 'appear' to be so.

That so–called privileges or the advantages of birth, education, race or country are largely non–existent: that each and every person, in the end, if not at the beginning, can, and does, break even. I would have no belief at all in the Creator, God, Nature, Infinite Spirit, call it what you will, if this All trafficked in 'favourites' – specially 'chosens' even saved or unsaved. I will have none of it.

I do admit freely, frankly and fully, that we are not all born equal in graces, brains or ability, but I do affirm that no power exists, human or superhuman, that opposes the genuine aspirations and sincere attempts of any personality to advance itself.

On the contrary, I affirm that our destiny is in our own hands. No one but a fool would deny that we do find difficulties, set–backs, frustrations, even inevitabilities, at times, and by dozens – hundreds.

But I never did admit that patience, intelligence, persistence, in the end, will fail to find a way round, through, or over, any difficulty with which each or any one of us may be confronted.

For God, or the Infinite Power, never submits any individual to any ordeal, task or problem without also providing the means or solution for the overcoming.

Because weakly types and false doctrines would have you

believe the opposite is merely a test of your intelligence, and the power of your own personality.

It is true the weak cleave to the weak, and believe all manner of extraordinary things – but, believe me, if you have read thus far you are little likely to lack the brains or understanding to solve all your own personal problems, and achieve, in time, all the reasonable ambitions that may rest in your secret heart.

Because there may be many who will dispute what I say means little or nothing to me. The advancing personality, the will–to–win person, athlete, he will take fresh heart from my message, my words. The rest never did count, anyway, although they can have a nuisance value.

The second great fallacy is that there are any special heavens, states or hereafters either in this world or any hypothetical next. I am an apostle of the *now* – the everlasting *present.* Do today all you *reasonably* can – in your training, your affairs.

Do not attempt to see the end of the road. Keep your 'ends' or goals in *mind*, but direct your brains to the solving and satisfactorily doing of all that your hands, or feet, find to do today.

Restrain the propensity, in all of us today – to dream – imagine what we will do, what we will become.

It is true that imagination is an essential quality, but not when it stops at just imagining ourselves great athletes, or successful persons, and entirely lacks the normal next step – *action* – the getting up and doing – in the rain, in the heat, in the cold, in the dark! Unless you are one of the 'doers' you are destined to remain unknown, unsung, unhonoured as an athlete or man. In a word, you will not count much.

Maybe, you may say – *that* suits you. *That* is O.K. with me. I have always found the heights of our mountains, the 'tops' in anything, are not distinguished by being cluttered up by 'no–hopers'. It just does not happen: they just do not get there – probably do not want to.

Such people, 'the valley folk', have a place in the scheme and affairs of the world – it is not for me to criticize or condemn.

But I do address myself to the young man – and woman, too – who *would* achieve: who look longingly, and honestly, at the heights and 'tops'.

To them, I say – go on in faith. You *can* achieve them – the 'way' *does* open up. The way–showers *are* there in your emergencies: your *genuine* needs.

You may feel you walk, or travel, 'the way' alone – but it is only the darkness of our minds that makes us feel this.

We soon find we march along in quite a goodly company – the company of those destined to be great – to get somewhere – to become something. Do not think for one moment that *you* have to run a world record to be honoured amongst the greatest. If you *do* feel that way, then you have already forgotten the story of Fricker.

Fricker set no world records, at least, on the record books – he never got down to four minutes or 1:50 nor even fourteen minutes, but he *did* achieve fame – undying fame – at Portsea, and maybe you may say: What of that! What's Portsea!

This *is* true. What *is* Portsea? Who *is* Cerutty?

But maybe the story of Fricker may turn the tide in some greatly gifted athlete who may eventually run 3:50 for the mile, or 12:55 for three miles, or nine seconds for the 100.

This is not impossible. Therefore the *spirit* of Fricker may never die: may help inspire someone to great deeds, maybe some athlete, even, at Portsea, sleeping in the same bunk as the Landys, the Stephens, the Macmillans, the Hendersons, the Halbergs, the Thomases, the Baillies, the Elliotts – all of whom have run four minutes for the mile, as I write, or close enough to it that it does not matter. Curiously enough, there is such a bunk – the most cramped and lesser of the four bunks – in the hut.

This is just one example of how the truly great will take what is left – the least and last, in the things that do not count – and are able to grasp and hold the things that do count.

I can tell them, the great ones and the lesser greats.

The 'lessers' tend to rush in and grab the best – always. The 'greater' greats stroll in without hurry and accept what is left – in the things that do not really count. So it was with the bunks. The 'greats' are left with cramped 'uppers'.

However, this bunk, in our little life here, has become famous, at least locally. So – who knows what young athlete sleeping peacefully and soundly after his day's training and efforts may dream as he sleeps of great deeds, also – and he is a brave man indeed who can assert with certainty that the spirit of these Australian and New Zealand athletes may not pass into our young athletic tyro.

Such is my 'naturism' that I have always felt that some such spirit does cling to even the inanimate things of life – and I can affirm that the Spirit of the Great Ones *does* enter into us – and inspire and support us much more than we may realize.

I know that such has been the case in my own experience. The spirit of the living and the dead.

If you can view the masterpieces of Michelangelo and da Vinci, of Bellini and so many more: If you can hear the music of Bach and Beethoven, Rossini and Verdi: If you can look upon the busts of Julius Caesar and Einstein, in London, as I have done: If you can stand and see, and feel, the wonders of it all, *everywhere* – in the woods, the mountains, the museums – *everywhere*: If you can tread the deck of the *Endeavour* with Scott's ghost, in Norway sit with the spirit of Amundsen, or upon the raft that drifted across the Pacific: If you can meet the Zatopeks, the Kutses, the Peters and McKenleys and Connollys and be greeted by them: If you can *feel* you have helped just someone else to do something a little better: If you can feel all this, surely you can feel the spirit of these great ones pass into you, and you know, as we all must – I, 'of myself, am nothing'.

Truly is it said, but so little understood, that the last shall be first, and those that are lifted up humbled; and those who are despised – the little ones of great heart – it is they, perhaps, who gain the greatest rewards; for there *are* greater rewards than Olympic Games Gold Medals, and awards for this and awards for that – the greatest honours that can be conferred.

There is the recognition by, the acceptance by, the fraternity of the truly great, those who judge and recognize their equals – not so much by their *results* as by their *strivings:* not so much by what they *won*, but what they *did:* not so much by what they *were*, but by what they *became*.

So, I say, take heart. It is not given to every man to be a Zatopek, but it *can* be given to many to be a Fricker – and in the annals of the Truly Great many names occur that the little people – the doubters and disparagers – never dream of as being on the list. All the 'heroes' of the world do not necessarily wear the V.C. or the ribbon of the Legion, or what–have–you.

But they *are* known – where it counts!

It is in true humbleness of spirit that we recognize – all of us – that we tread in the footsteps of those who have gone before.

Let us be worthy of them – so that they would not, their ghosts and spirits, pass us in the gloom – the lonely gloom of the great ones – yes, it is *not* quite what the young ones may imagine it, being great – but, as I say, let it never be said that the Spirit of the Great Ones would turn sadly away from us, in that day, because we failed to 'go *on*', because we quit: we didn't *really* try!

We are *truly* judged by them, never by ourselves, much less our contemporaries.

Be content in this, you who would be great. Posterity will judge you – some day – truly.

But it is only *you* who can place yourself in the niche of 'worthiness', of Fame – if *that* fickle dame is she whom you would woo!

For truly *success can be yours!*

CHAPTER 9

Many may yet ask: Why all this emphasis upon athleticism? Why bother to become a champion? *This* is to tell you why!

Athleticism, in my view, is not a sport: nor a cult: it is a *way of life*. For me, and those like me, the only *basic* way of life. In my day, I have tried many things – and from all I turned away, eventually, to return to athleticism. The term 'athleticism' does not merely imply running and field games, not at all.

It means, to me, *all* activities that are based in sweat and effort – and are something *added* to our normal, ordinary everyday way of life.

Athleticism *can* be a profession: a whole-time job. It loses nothing, perhaps, by being so – since, certainly, it is my prime enthusiasm, although I have never, as yet, been able to live on, or by, it.

But many successful gymnasts, wrestlers, cyclists and the like, do.

They are *all* men. One cannot be tops in such activities and be a 'little' man, puny in strength and spirit.

Indeed, I will go so far as to say that it is only the athletes, in this broad sense, who truly 'live': who can savour life in all its aspects. And being fit, being an athlete, in no way debars one from being a poet, an artist, a musician, a great sportsman in the sense that a golfer is a philosopher, scientist, academician, or a successful business man.

We have not arrived at the day, yet, when all that I have mentioned is found, also, in athletes. More is the pity. When that day does arrive – when our politicians are athletes as well as – well, politicians – I opine all the world's troubles will be over: our waste on wars, our mass stupidities, fears, superstitions and childlike behaviour, in general. For only the fit are fearless. Only those who feel the strength in their muscle cells have *true* confidence. Only those who excel in something physical, but yet exercise the mind, can ever hope to be balanced: to *live* balanced lives.

And balance, equilibrium, is the first law of the Universe; without it we have no law, no order, nothing.

Can it be said that a man who is all brain, a man with a diseased or weakly body, is likely to have a sane and balanced outlook? Would you have confidence in your aeroplane pilot if you knew he was unfit, about to have a 'stroke' – had high blood pressure, suffered from kidney fits?

No matter what his I.Q., what certificates and diplomas he carried, sensible people would seek another plane and pilot.

Yet we entrust the Ship of State to such people. Our leaders in all walks of life – our journalists (who make up our minds for us), our teachers, our successful(?) men in all walks of life – what are they?

Mostly only partly fit – if fit at all. Few are *men* – in *every* sense of the word. Most, after fifty, could not propagate their own species. Useless, except to dominate through power: cowardly – so must control us all, they tell us, for our sakes. I will have none of them.

The fit, the truly strong, active, positive men who are athletes do not *feel* the need, the many supports and ramifications, that the weakly feel they must bolster themselves up with. The strong and fit do not fear the other man, the other country, their competitor, as do the weakly.

The athlete *lives* now, right at this moment – he is *alive,* he functions. He has little or no concern with hereafters, heavens, even futures in this life – he is too busy living in the everlasting present. He senses and feels that the past is dead – why fret about it: that the future – it, with all its anticipated worries, hopes and fears – may never happen: may never be realized.

The athlete, possibly with the artist, *lives* in the *now*, and extracts from it *all* that living suggests and presents to us.

It is true, in the past, there has been a tendency to consider the athlete a man without superior intelligence – an uneducated, physically strong oaf. There are 'superior' people today who still pretend to such nonsense, who shelter their weakly attitudes behind such conceits. The truth is that slowly, maybe, those of superior intelligence, as opposed to 'brains', are recognizing the importance of fitness, health and strength.

What profits a man if he 'makes a million' and ends up a hypochondriac, or is dead at fifty! The dead make no love, run no miles, scale no mountains, hear no symphonies, look at no pictures, eat no oats!

For countless millions of years, until the last few centuries, most men have earned their bread by labour. Even in the last centuries, and to this day, men sweat. It is almost impossible, in my view, to be fit and fearless (the two words are synonymous) without some sweating exercise – most days.

The brain, that organ of cunning plots and plans, is too young an organ in our evolvement to be relied upon – yet. It is self-evident that it *does not* protect us – as we fondly hope and imagine. Despite its vaunted abilities, it does let us develop dropsy, the staggers, grow fat, become alcohol and nicotine addicts. It *does not* protect us from unhappiness, from our wives leaving us – or prevent them and everyone else battening upon us until we wish we were more dead than we are – or they are!

I tell you, only the fit, the athlete who has taken his fitness along as the companion of his agedness, can truly buck them all – the tax-gatherer, the politician, the 'mad-managers' – off his back and still smile – enigmatically perhaps, but still amused by it all – the wild scrambles for wealth and power, the fears and horrors at the thought of the losses.

Only the fit, the strong, athlete feels in any emergency that he will survive, if anyone does; that he will not starve when all around may be starving; that he can protect his loved ones if need be, since he feels that ways and means are his – despite what others may say, claim or deride.

It is true the young will not be very interested in such serious views; but the 'intelligent' young will be.

Whilst Nature favours the fit, it is 'high intelligence' that causes us to want to be fit. Therefore fitness and high intelligence can be considered one.

Death ever awaits the stupid, since fools *do* rush in, and in time only the fit and intelligent ones and their heirs will inherit the earth. It may take a few centuries – a millennium even, but in time all the weakly, the foolish, the vain and the ignorant *must* pass away. The process is at work *now*! The foolish young men who *die* – no matter what heroes they are deemed: they have no sons. War and disease, drugs and mental sickness, in the end kill off the foolish and the weakly.

It is still the survival of the 'fittest'. It always will be. Fitness and intelligence being synonymous in my view.

So we come to athleticism as a *sensible* attitude, not merely a sporting one. And it sure pays dividends – this fitness, this *joie de vivre*, this living business, whether it be at twenty, thirty, forty, fifty or sixty.

I cannot speak, personally, as to the seventy, eighty and ninety levels – but I am planning in that direction, yes, sir!

What is valuable to the young especially? I shall list them:

1. *Knowing* they are adult: *feeling* they are – men.
2. *Enjoying* the respect of those around them, especially those above them in age and/or position.

3. The ability to carve their own careers: make their own way: seize what they feel they are reasonably entitled to.
4. To *feel* strong, muscularly, and to be able to act as strong men.
5. To conquer, to overcome, to be able to demonstrate these abilities.
6. To rise up to positions of self-satisfaction, to be 'champions' in something, even if only just *one* thing.
7. To believe and know they can wrest a livelihood for themselves and those dependent upon them by their own two hands alone, if necessary.

One does not have to set world records to know and feel what I have listed. But it is important that you have lived and strived, trained and disciplined yourself as if you had set world records.

The setting of the record, or any record, even a *personal* one – is of no real consequence, except as *evidence* of something. That something is the knowledge of accomplishment: of power within us: of a job well done.

I believe: that in the future it will be recognized that we can have no *true* spiritual or mental values without the results accruing to the personality from well-balanced fitness and athleticism in some form.

That no *true* aesthetic values can be arrived at, or appreciated, without the fitness and attitudes of the intellectually developed athlete.

Chapter 10

Something on food: ailment: diet. The three words mean the same

This is not so much to tell the athlete what he should eat, as to tell him what we eat at Portsea, and what *principles* govern our food and its intake.

It would be as foolish to lay down definite rules in these matters of food as it is foolish to lay down definite rules for the training and conditioning of athletes.

There are so many variables that a common rule, applicable to all races, types, events, climates, customs and the like, makes the whole subject unreal, just as laying down in detail the place, speed, distances to be run, is as equally unreal as those who attempt to train in such a manner have come to realize.

By their deeds do we know them.

Athletes who find pleasure in, or are even able to subject themselves to, the dictations of an authority: who, without questioning, find they easily submit to these things – such athletes must learn that they will be limited just so much as they submit.

So it is with food: the 'principles' will apply in every country, for every race, in all climates; but the details as to the aliment may vary very considerably.

So let us set down what we do *not* like at Portsea, and give what sensible reasons we can to justify our likes and dislikes.

Firstly, we do not like animal fats. Even the domestic animals, the cats and the dogs, will not eat animal fat – some would rather starve, I have noticed. It *is* true some 'pets' have been educated away from even their natural instincts, so that here in Australia we do hear of dogs that will not eat raw meat – their meat must be cooked. But, believe me, these pampered pets have nothing in common with the farmer's dogs, accustomed, as they may be, to having to run down a rabbit, tear it out of its furry coat, and consume it on the spot, or go hungry.

We are *not* vegetarians, but I say that we *could* be, perhaps *should* be. But we do not rely upon meat of any kind at all for *strength*. What meat we do eat, and we eat very little beef or mutton, is because we believe we need protein to replace body tissue wastage.

We believe that this tissue wastage goes on at a steady rate irrespective of our output in the form of exercise, so we do not bump up the intake of protein because we may step up our exertions.

We all believe 'mixed' proteins may prove to be better than purely animal form. So we eat our protein in the form of what is found in grain (oats, mostly), nuts, cheese (a little daily), eggs (one or two daily, raw or lightly cooked), poultry and fish, which we prefer to beef or mutton.

We make sure our intake is ample, relying on the excess being from the vegetarian sources rather than the animal sources, which, in excess, tend to putrefy in the intestinal tract.

I seem to have read that in countries where the incidence of meat consumption is low, and the incidence of vegetarianism is high, there also the incidence of cancer is low, and that, to me, in this age of a high incidence in our country of deaths from cancerous growths, is rather significant. I personally prefer to take no chances.

Also, I hold, as our 'nature' becomes refined, thoughtful, considerate, we can hardly justify with complacency the realities as they apply to trafficking in animals for food. The thought is not a pleasant one and those fastidious eaters, especially, who stick their artificials into some choice steak or kidney, may have a different outlook if they visited the charnel houses called abattoirs – and spent a day assisting in some of the duties done daily by men – who are the husbands and fathers of someone – mostly.

I look forward to an age – not in my time, of course – when mankind turns from such bestialities. In the meantime I am weakly complaisant – I admit – and am prepared to be condemned for this attitude by my more humanitarian and vegetarian brothers whom I respect muchly.

But I will say this in my self-defence, if any be needed: I do not require the meats of animals. I *was* a strict vegetarian (a lacto-vegetarian, there is a distinction here) for many years. I do not like and seldom eat meat in the usual form – other than sausage – but I am weak enough, and illogical enough, to confess to enjoying a little fish and fowl occasionally.

My 'boys' – the few athletes who grow up round me – soon become the same as I am – since they *must*. It is no use clamouring for huge steaks at Portsea! And they soon learn the stupidity of imagining that a steak before racing is the ideal diet; it is the worst possible, really.

So we eschew animal fats, preferring vegetable oils – such as olive oil, especially, or peanut oil, or maize oil – which we use in cooking. Olive oil is costly here, so we use it mostly for salad dressings.

And we are almost, but not quite, lacto-vegetarians. A lacto-vegetarian, for those unacquainted with the term, is one who does not eat meat as such, but does not reject the product of animals, such as milk, eggs and cheese.

I believe we would be just as well on nuts for proteins, but since variety *is* the spice of eating, as well as of life generally, we like variety – and usually manage to get what we like!

For those statistically minded, the intake of protein can be satisfied for an average-sized man, say 10 stone 6 lb., i.e. 150 lb. body weight, in three-quarters of a pound of meats daily, or two or three large eggs – or one-third of a pound of mild cheese.

We make up this total by something of each, *never the lot*; and rely on knowing we are getting ample protein by the addition of nuts, etc. We believe that the closer to Nature our food is, the better it is for us. Closer to Nature means – as we find it in Nature – out in the gardens, fields, the woods and the sea.

That means raw, unadulterated, unrefined, unprocessed.

I would say that if we were consistent – which we are not – we would eat *all* our food raw, and be better for it – if we were not poisoned in the process!

With beef measles, hydatids in animals, tuberculosis in milk, poisonous sprays on our lentils and crops, we have perforce to act carefully and kill our microbes and bacteria before consumption by submitting them to the heat of cooking. In doing so we destroy many of the vitamins; we know this and try to make up for this wasteful deficiency in other ways.

But what we can eat raw we reasonably do – we prefer our vegetables raw in salad forms, our carrots, tender cabbage leaves, onions and the like.

We prefer our fruits as we find them, in the garden and orchard, ripe and raw – rather than in preserves and jams – although we eat jam as well as honey, treacle, etc., on occasion.

Even our grains we prefer raw. In our country wheat is the main cereal, but it is a notoriously poor one, due to soil deficiencies. It is milled and refined until the resulting flour is almost useless, nothing but the starch being left. This is made into a white bread loaf; surely the poorest manufactured anywhere in the wide world. We avoid it. We eat it only under duress: fancied starvation. Indeed, we are not big bread-eaters – and what bread we do eat we try to ensure is the best type of wholemeal and rye breads.

We prefer oats in the form of rolled oats. Nothing is removed from the oat but the outer husk. Grown in Australia, I can well imagine it to be somewhat deficient in nutrients, as is our wheat – but, in this matter, beggars, or Australians, must be content with what the farmer and the Government give us. We grow our wheat for profit, not for food; and, truly, if we could get by with a poorer quality than what it is – and a bigger profit come out of it – that's us! The oats we usually grow for horses, and insist upon a better quality! We even import our best oats for our best horses!

Who cares two hoots about quality – or dying, or athletes, or children – as long as the national trade balance is favourable? No, sir! Not we Australians, anyhow!

So we munch our oats hopefully, knowing that they are, even if not 100 per cent, at least 90 per cent, superior to what I call the manufactured monstrosities packed, and publicly consumed, under the name of breakfast cereals.

Fortunes have been made by the manufacturers of these cereals – and the undertakers – but we do not care to assist either. Indeed, our object is to cheat the latter of his job as long as we possibly can – and would walk, or run, to our own funerals if that feat were humanly possible.

Neither do we think it impossible to train or work unless we start the day with heavy protein foods – or even the traditional bacon and eggs.

We may eat these things for breakfast – but only because of hunger – or a whim, almost. We try to be governed by our needs, hungers, rather than artificially cultivated appetites.

Appetite can be cultivated for anything 'tasty'. *Hunger* is usually satisfied with anything 'handy'. We make a distinction here.

We avoid 'tasty' dishes: sauces, spices, appetite-whetters.

We are, not hungry if we do not rush in and start seeking the oatmeal bag, the dried fruits and the nuts – at breakfast-time.

Breakfast is a free-for-all. No set hour. We eat when hungry. No man normally is hungry, or should be, on rising. So we work, or exercise, run or swim for an hour or so on getting up – then we eat. Raw rolled oats, dried fruits, raisins, sultanas and the like, nuts. We prefer walnuts, since they are softer.

Quantity? Some of the voracious boys eat huge bowlfuls; a bowl six inches in diameter and four inches deep not being unusual. They sit in the sun or around the stove and steadily and manfully munch their way through this food. It takes twenty to thirty minutes. It is eaten dry, no milk or honey being needed. Saliva does its proper job at Portsea.

Occasionally – when *very* hungry – we may eat, after the oats, or those who eat smaller quantities of the oats, thick brown bread, with or 'without margarine, plastered with vegemite, jam or honey, according to taste. We are not 'purists' at Portsea. Some would say – savages, rather! Be sure, however, we are natural, happy and strong, whatever else our defects or lacks.

Or someone may chip some potatoes in oil, poach or fry (in oil) some eggs, or fish. It's a free-for-all, and all are encouraged to eat as they feel. We soon find that the visitor makes up his mind, *positively*, in these matters, when he decides to have chip potatoes and eggs, or toast, *after* his oats – and he finds he has to prepare the potatoes, find the eggs – or toast the bread.

Nothing, *we* find, is more conducive to making clean and clear-cut decisions between appetite and hunger, those two inseparables than having to prepare the food for oneself. How often do we hear then, 'I do not think I shall bother, thank you!' – and thus both the pantry and the stomach are profited thereby.

Breakfast is usually around 9 a.m. at Portsea. Business, etc., away from Portsea, of course, dominates our lives, programmes and time-tables. Business is king in Australia, as elsewhere. As he is mostly in league with the undertaker – and the heart specialist – we would get along with as little as possible to do with any of them. This is only possible at Portsea – but even that helps, be it only weekends.

Some of us look forward to a millennium in this and spend much time in trying to persuade our governments to reform themselves and us. We fail, of course. So much so that we suspect all our great authorities, governmental bodies and institutions are secretly, at least, big shareholders in the numerous hospital institutions, 'sleeping' partners (this is not meant to be facetious) of the physicians – and, of course, profit-sharing partners of our morticians and funeral directors – rapidly becoming one of our main and biggest business institutions, and most profitable, I hear.

In this regard I honestly knew one very financially successful man who 'got it both ways', as he told me. He ran a very big and profitable hotel, dispensing alcohol to his clients, and round the corner he had the town's most successful and busy mortician parlours. I cannot say for certain, but I think his son was a doctor (a physician), so that the whole enterprise of life and death was kept in the family.

There is one catch in all this – we *can* run out of customers. I prefer to cheat the lot of them. I am indifferent as to their privations, even to their bankruptcies. I have no conscience or remorse in this. Truly are we heartless and ruthless at Portsea.

So we work or train all mornings on the beaches, in the surf, at the track – and when tired and hungry we return – and eat again. This is usually about 2 p.m. And the meal – *a la carte*, often alfresco (taken to the beaches). Salads are the rule; anything and everything that can be eaten raw: some fish, such as herrings; cheeses or similar, to make it tasty; wholemeal bread. Milk is taken at this meal, one pint per athlete.

The table is loaded with the viands – covered with a net to exclude any odd flies (we have few, if any, since they are mostly attracted by the smell of putrefaction) – and the hungry ones come in and eat.

This meal is a light one – and afterwards we mostly take a short siesta. Around 4 or 5 p.m. the activity recommences: training, conditioning, swimming; and the main meal of the day arrives around 7 or 8 p.m. This consists of a protein food, mostly fish or fowl, eggs or some other form of protein – meat, ample potatoes, baked in the oven, or chipped in oil – vegetables conservatively cooked with a little water, enough only to prevent burning. The liquid residue from the cooking, usually less than half a pint, is as avidly sought and consumed as nectar would be. There is no limit placed upon the consumption of this food. Healthy lads and athletes need bulk as well as quality of food.

As long as the bulk is in the form of vegetables, positively no harm can come from the quantity consumed – and they will only eat in conformity with *hunger* – not appetite, we find. Should this food not be enough there is always a good thick slice or two of wholemeal bread to fill in the crevices; milk, half a pint each athlete, is taken with this meal. The sweet is universally fruit salad, and the cream, the top of the milk, whipped up. No additional cream is ever bought or used. We feel the reasonable balance is somehow better maintained this way.

Between meals, but not before the expiration of two hours, we drink – copiously, I hope. Water is cheap and pure here. We use it plentifully.

We take tea, we weak ones, twice daily – on rising and before dinner at night. Not everyone. Oh, no – just the weaker, the *more* elderly, the socially inclined.

As a treat we have a little wine also. But it is not encouraged or customary. We never indulge in nicotine: *that* killer *is* barred at Portsea. I suppose we have to be a kill-joy in something. So we fixed on 'Nerve-sticks' and we call those weak and foolish enough to be nicotine addicts 'Lung-o's' since we know what their lungs *must* be.

Nicotine is a 'heart-kicker', a 'cough-coffiner', and can find no place at all in the serious athlete's life – nor is it needed by *real* men – who must intellectually as well as instinctively regard it with the keenest suspicion.

Personally, I do not feel this way about the moderate use of alcohol. But *that* is not necessary in the life of the young athlete either.

To be precise, at Portsea the one is 'tabooed', the other 'not encouraged'.

We never eat suppers. We do not eat between meals. We do not drink with our food: milk coagulates into a semi-solid in the stomach and is considered a food, not a beverage.

We drink water, or tea, before eating. Water especially, passes out of the stomach immediately. We prefer food we must use our teeth upon rather than soft foods such as custards, although we occasionally have such.

We never eat the refined, manufactured product of any form, and as little as possible out of tins or jars. We are not food faddists, we hope, and drink sugar with our tea, without worrying whether it is tinted brown or is completely denatured as it is – maybe we would be better without our few odd spoonfuls – we'll take a chance on that one.

We know our food is not perfect, so we take added vitamins in the form of the B complex, C & E especially, and a little of all the others occasionally. We are not regular and strict as to this. We eat wheat-germ – when we think of it – malt and cod liver oil, when we remember to, and crude molasses, when we want to punish ourselves.

We enjoy our food – immensely, we feel – but we eat to live, rather than what we suspect is the order for the many.

In the winter we may make hot thick porridge for some and a thick vegetable and barley and meat soup for additional fortification.

There may be other odd items that come in occasionally, but I cannot recollect them offhand. We eat little or no salt – that is in the main an unnecessary addiction. If you eat mostly salads and drink the vegetable water you do not seem to need salt – and we never use peppers or mustard. Little in the way of appetizers or sauces. But a meat spaghetti dish is a favourite, although we know it is not 'perfect', but then, neither are we.

We eat shellfish of all kinds, when we can afford it.

On the whole there is little or nothing 'natural', and in Nature, that we despise or do not like. Those who come here soon lose their fads – likes and dislikes. We impose nothing – it just happens, we find.

We never need medicines, aperients, nor does anyone suffer from indigestion, colds or constipation. Mostly we are too 'disgustingly' fit, as it has been termed. We do not make a fetish of anything – our food or our training. We have no set rules or times – nothing is forced or prescribed. But we all follow a common routine. We find, in our weekends at least, we are self-sufficient. We have our radiogram, and good music, or calypso, pours out in a constant stream it is true – but the folk are young – even the sixty-year-olds! Indeed, none of our women ever seem to go beyond the 'fair' forties, and the men stick for ever, it would appear, in the six-minute sixties.

Our physician is the poorest man in the district – he runs a bulldozer as a sideline – and the mortician went out of business years ago. He just gave up – and joined us, and now builds houses for our numerous and increasing progeny: not mine, I hasten to add, but the young athletes', who set themselves up – happily and healthily, as all young men and women should – first as 'lovers *for* life', as well as lovers *of* life. We aim at both!

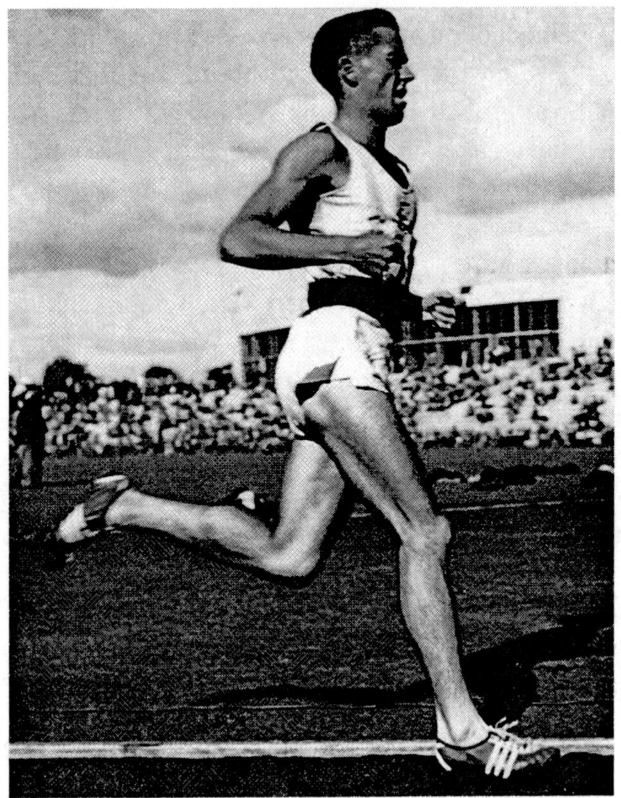

Albert Thomas

One year prior to the Olympic Games in Melbourne, Thomas was not considered a possibility, except by myself and his own hopefulness, as a competitor. Yet Thomas won a place in the Australian team to compete in the 5,000 metres event, won his heat with a beautiful exhibition of front running in perfect form, and , despite his inexperience and youth, went on to run a meritorious fifth place in the final: the best ever by an Australian.

Said to be handicapped by lack of inches, Thomas measures only five feet five inches tall, this pocket athletic giant went on a year or so later to run second in the British Empire Games three mile, set new world records for the two mile and three mile run, and in a mile run at Dublin returned 3:58.6, a time that equalled the Australian mile record that stands to this time of writing to John Landy. So much for 'too small'.

Above: Free play at Portsea. This picture shows the kind of activities that help to enliven the athletes' day. Mostly this kind of horse-play starts up on the sand of the beach, when it may happen that someone is tossed into the sea, or sat upon by some half-dozen hairy, sweaty stalwarts.

Below: A study of coach and pupil

Chapter 11

My views on weight-conditioning for athletes, runners in particular, although I would say my views apply equally to the needs of field games exponents. Some criticism of the authorities mostly accepted

I shall deal with my criticism first in order to prepare the way for my own views.

Firstly, I know of no one, other than myself; who at one and the same time was deeply interested in, and strenuously practised, both weight-conditioning for weight-lifting and competitive running over middle distance and distances up to the marathon.

This I was doing as long ago as 1947. At this time I was training in running up to 200 miles per month, considered a big mileage in those days, and lifting heavy weights some three times weekly, often daily. During this period I have moved as much as 70,000 foot-pounds in dead-lifting in a day's workout. In running I would run up to as much as twenty-five miles on occasion, even more.

I would support my connection with both these sports by stating that at this time I was Senior Vice-President of the Victorian Weight-lifting Association and Vice-President of the Malvern Harriers Club.

I claim also to be the first authority of any note, am I permitted to say, to advocate strongly the use of the barbell for the strengthening of athletes (runners) who I noticed were mostly very weak in their upper body development. This I did in articles published in Australia and in Britain, as well as in privately issued material.

However, apart from applying the principles to my own development, some fifteen years ago I commenced applying the aims and methods to certain young athletes not too prejudiced to try out my, then, revolutionary and universally condemned advocacy of heavy-weight resistance conditioning.

The first of these young athletes was one John Pottage, aged twenty years. A student with no background of exercise or sport, six feet three inches in height, some 130 lb. in weight, young Pottage had been rejected in the Army call-up because of sub-standard physique. Here was an ideal type. Within three years Pottage had strengthened himself to the order that he was engaged in heavy labouring work and had become a State Champion runner and record-holder over distances from three miles to twenty miles, running twenty miles in 1:53 53, a then Australian record.

John Pottage was closely followed by Leslie Perry, Warren, Macmillan and, later, Landy, amongst those who became Australian, or world, record runners. David Stephens, holder of the world record, was also of this period, but his record run came much later, in 1955.

Landy was never a great enthusiast for very strenuous work of an *intensive* nature, either of running or body-conditioning, preferring more *extensive* work than what I have always advocated. It is a truism to say that Landy's career would have been greater had he trained along intensive lines, rather than extensive lines. In justice to Landy it is fair to state that he probably approached his personal problems as to training from the intrinsic nature peculiar to him, as we all tend to do if not subjected to outside direction. I can state in support of my contentions that John Landy is known to have said that he regrets not having trained in his running more intensively, and with his weight-condition, with heavier and more intensive exercises, although I can personally testify that John made himself quite above average strength in the arms and upper body.

Stephens, however, acquired a much heavier set of weights, and these, together with his daily work of handling heavy milk crates, made Dave a very strong man at his body weight.

Just how much this strengthening lifted Australian athletes from a poor mediocrity to world class can never be truly appraised. But no other Australian athlete was comparable to my group at that time.

Athletes like Herb Elliott, nineteen years, 4:00.4 mile, are being conditioned to a far tougher regime than the earlier champions I have named above. We can but wait and see the results that are expected to ensue.[1]

Most authorities on weight-conditioning for athletes (runners) appear to me to base their opinions as to the needs of runners upon their experience in the one sport only, viz. weight-lifting. This seems to have led to the erroneous conclusion that runners do not need to be strength-conditioned with the same poundages as may be applied to the weight-lifter, body-weight as to body-weight; initial strength to strength. Although it is now recorded that more than one great athlete has also been a competing weight-lifter.

Then we have the running enthusiast, with no knowledge, or but the scantiest, of the iron game, who has presumed to imagine what weight-conditioning involves, the principles behind it, and who has prescribed ridiculously low weights, many repetitions, and placed emphasis upon the speed of the movements.

The last category of 'authorities' contains some quite well known and approved in athletics. Some of these people have had no first-hand, or little, experience of either running or lifting, and have 'guessed' as best they might, or adopted the views of others that appeared to suit best.

Before the matter of authorities can be finally disposed of we must consider the qualified users of weight resistance themselves. These are, broadly, in two well-defined classes, viz, the body-conditioners and the weight-lifters. The body-conditioners, primarily, are not concerned with the sport of moving very heavy weights in appropriate movements, for competitive purposes, but with developing the 'body magnificent'. This puts size and muscular definition before strength proper. Their objective is competitions based in 'appearance' such as the universal 'Mr' competitions. Those not so ambitious aim merely at a good physique – a not unworthy aim by any means.

To achieve the aims of these 'body-builders' a technique has been evolved that 'blows' up the muscles, since great size is the chief objective. It has been found that muscles worked with heavy weights and many repetitions, especially until very 'hot', grow big. The weights used are not as heavy as those customarily used by the 'lifters' and the 'reps' tend to be much more extensive. Such men tend to become both big and strong, but seldom the strongest; indeed, for their bulk, many are comparatively weak when compared with a champion weightlifter. Perhaps in the order of two as to three; or three as to four.

The practising 'lifter', however, approaches his problem in a different manner. Firstly, his problem is to obtain greater strength without any appreciable gain in size or body-weight, since if he moves into a higher body-weight class he might easily defeat his objective, which is to be a champion lifter in his class, and not necessarily big or imposing.

So the lifter, to achieve his ends, viz, strength without any appreciable gain in bulk, has evolved a different technique to that of the 'body-builder'. He works with maximum weights, and this alone ensures that his 'reps' are reduced to a minimum, often only two or three.

This approach necessarily reduces the time he can apply himself to his exertions. His training then is intensive, just as the body-builder tends to train *extensively*.

The intensive system is known to alter the nature of the muscle fibre – and to strengthen it – rather than get added strength by increased size of muscle. Some of the results are startling, I might add.

I follow and advocate the *intensive* system. Most or all other authorities on the needs of runners tend to advocate the extensive system. I hold that the runner, above all others, perhaps, needs 'light' steely muscles rather than bulky, weighty ones.

The runner is not concerned with size of muscle, but of quality. Perhaps two of the greatest, Herb McKenley, and now Herb Elliott, are notoriously thin in the legs in comparison with even non-athletes. Yet McKenley in his day, and Elliott in his, will prove the greatest of their era.

Naturally enough I have little other than pity or contempt for those who hope to acquire strength by the use of light weights and puny efforts. I think it even worse that 'authorities' should advocate such practices. To me their concepts are puerile, their ends poor, their achievements lack reality, knowledge, even 'manliness'.

To me it could be laughable if it was not so pitiable, that grown men are told to handle weight in the order of twenty-five pound for presses, to jump while they do the exercise, or to lift as low as thirty-five pounds in the dead-lift.

I immediately set the veriest novice on his body-weight for the dead-lift, and what he can move six times, but not ten times, becomes his starting weight for any exercise other than the dead-lift.

And they increase the weight to be moved as soon as they can handle the exercise weight ten times on most days. Three 'reps' of ten of the determined weight for each exercise will soon develop any runner to a strength quite sufficient to his needs as a runner. He will be said to have approached that strength when he hoists his own body-weight over his head by any means he cares to adopt.

The most erroneous doctrine in the matter of weight work is that slower, heavy work makes the athlete sluggish; that fast, quick movements make him quicker. The doctrine is false. There are some naturally ponderous men; they rarely try to become runners.

Those who are attracted to athletics are usually naturally nimble and active. Enhanced strength makes them more so. Great strength, properly acquired, makes for quicker reflexes, greater agility, longer stride, more endurance (since great strength can be parcelled out in a short terrific effort – or a longer easier one).

Summed up, the whole purpose of weight-conditioning, as any form of conditioning such as running the sandhill, is to acquire enhanced 'power' in order that we can do a thing more powerfully, faster, better.

As I have briefly shown, the technique is known and has been practised for generations, and was perfectly known in the days of the great George Hackenschmidt, around the turn of the century. It has been the basis of the work of the greatest gymnasts, tumblers and strongmen from time, almost, immemorial.

It is now used by golfers, tennis players, pole vaulters and other specialists, all who find they have greater control, resilience and power at their command.

Nothing could be more fallacious than the statement that weight-conditioned men become muscle bound, or slow in movement. Such charges have always been levelled by the puny types and the fearful. It is thus we know them!

Weaker types, and those who advocate watered down concepts, tend, by the very constitution of society, to attract a greater number of followers – the many being weak rather than strong, negative rather than positive. Again, it is how we know them.

Those with a 'big' outlook in the widest sense: those who

aim at the very top: those coaches and mentors capable of envisaging the means and the way to the top – the 'world-class' top – they will always have a limited appeal. So much so is this to me that if my views were generally acceptable, were received without general opposition, I would suspect them of being outmoded, obsolete. To me it is axiomatic; if it is traditional it is useless, outworn, suspect.

I rest content in my views for many reasons: I have achieved some personal success and success with others not notable for their gifts in any way in the beginning, and in more sports than running. I am still achieving successes, personal (if I may say so, at sixty-three years of age, as witness my recent 5:32 mile), and the feats of my most recent youthful athlete, Herb Elliott, who after four months' very hard conditioning moved from a mile best of 4:20 to 4:00.4, at the age of ten days over his nineteenth birthday, as well as a 1:49.2 880 yards – a best-ever by an Australian.

That my teachings may be rather for the exclusive few who would aim high I do not deny. As I dislike watering down my methods to suit the level of the weaker and more numerous ones, I never expect my views to be really popular. That which appeals to the many can never be exclusive. Championship and world-record class is rather exclusive still. Personally, I like it that way.

1 Elliott went on to establish world records for the mile and 1,500 metres and establish a record never excelled in six months' racing by any other athlete ever. How much his records and superior racing were due to his weight-conditioning is, of course, problematical, but it is very significant and surely more than coincidence.

CHAPTER 12

On conditioning and training: a general introduction

In practically every sport, athletics included, until recent years it was generally considered that the strength a sportsman, or athlete, found himself endowed with was the strength natural to him, and he expected to be limited by it in the practice of, or participation in, his chosen sport.

It was not considered necessary or advantageous to attempt to add to that strength. Indeed, any vigorous aids were frowned upon as not only disadvantageous but it was actually held that any such extra activities used up the precious available strength to the marked disadvantage of the sporting, or athletically, specialized goals or ambitions.

On the whole, big and strong types were looked upon as 'natural' footballers, oarsmen, wrestlers, etc.; whilst smaller or weaker types had to be content with poor–type competition, or seek satisfaction as 'distance runners' or, worse, no sport at all!

In practically all cases the actual limits to extra exercise or development were confined to walking, deep breathing exercises (now known to be harmful, by the way), calisthenics and moving two-pound dumbbells!

To lift very heavy weights, to desire to become strong, really strong, and well muscled, was not only considered inadvisable but positively harmful. 'Authorities', coaches and trainers spoke glibly of 'muscle-bound'; athletes were fearful of becoming 'too big', 'too strong' (believe it or not, in regard to the latter!), even that they might stride too long! and, of course, from the brains and expostulations of these authoritative ones came the catch-phrase – 'all brawn and no brains, meaning intellectually dull.

However, it is now being realized that power (physical strength) is the prime mover, that this power can be 'built-in', that greater strength makes for greater agility (skill), for endurance (because with greater strength we do a given task easier, therefore can continue longer).

It is also being increasingly realized that adventitious aids, such as the sandhill and the barbell, best provide this added power (strength), and is the factor, today, in the high speeds and superior performances, in all sports, of tomorrow. If we add, then, the gym rope, the horizontal bar, etc., and the mountain climb as essential aids to power, i.e. strength, we move to what I have been teaching and preaching for years.

We can best define conditioning by describing the activities that the advanced athlete has moved to today. Furthermore, by extending his interests and activities, widening his horizons, the athlete has introduced into his training regime factors that make for a wider, more interesting and varied life. This is how it should be.

As I have pointed out elsewhere, the pastime of athletics, especially when undertaken in the amateur spirit, should be one of strong masculine attitudes, health-giving and exhilarating, for both body and mind.

Perforce, the athlete who confines all his training to running round a track with occasional outings over the country must be limited in experience, variation, enjoyment and the development of strength (power) in comparison with the athlete who bases his training on regular visits to the weight-training venue, the gym, the coastal regions and hilly places, the sandhills, beaches, deserts and the high mountains.

What experiences, splendours, joys are his! And it all adds

up to power – the mental and physical power that is behind modern fast running (as we practise it)!

Power (strength) has always been behind fast running, long throwing, etc., although weak people prefer to dissect technique as if technique alone is all that is required to enable a weak man to run a mile in four minutes!

Technique is an important factor, but the best technique today is useless against the athlete who is supported by technique plus power (strength). The weaker ones can deny this; can chatter endlessly on this or that – analysing, pronouncing, dogmatizing – but unless they themselves can perform with power they will never know and will for ever be 'explaining' or decrying in the face of those whose efforts are superior.

It is true there is a compensation, a satisfaction, for everyone in life – the weakly as well as the strong. Just as there are levels of performance, of championships and standards, whether of performance or courage, spirit, intellectual approach and will.

It is not given to everyone to climb to the uttermost heights, nor descend to the uttermost depths – of suffering, effort, trial, but it is given to everyone to try and make the best of the material that is his, and decrying the stronger efforts and successes of our fellows, especially the depreciating and critical attitudes directed at those who would try to go higher, is one of the blasphemies, as I understand it.

So to conditioning.

Anything that conspires to make us stronger, freer, more resilient, conquering, all that trains us to endure, to sustain suffering, that calls on our best qualities, continually – is conditioning.

Whether one wishes to be a runner, field games exponent, footballer, tennis or golf player, whatever the sport, I hold the athlete is well advised, if he is able to do so, to spend six months of each year conditioning himself; i.e. making himself stronger, more active, vigorous, virile.

For a distance runner such as a miler, three-miler, he will spend approximately as many hours in other forms of conditioning as he will actually running.

For the sprinter the ratio could be 66:33 – 66 per cent being other than running activities and 33 per cent actual running; the marathon man would reverse this proportion, doing about 66 per cent of his available time and effort in conditioning by running and 33 per cent by conditioning in the gym, with barbells and other activities. (N.B. Mountain walking, swimming, occasional tennis, if played – any or all these activities are considered 'other than running'.)

But whatever his running may be, much of it will be hard.

Also I hold that running almost exclusively on flat or level surfaces, after an initial improvement, advances us little, particularly in reference to the time and mileage usually expended: This equally applies to doing free exercises without a heavy resistance. We build to a certain limited level, and there we stick. Little or no improvement is possible despite hours and years of continued effort. Really strong men, muscularly or as runners, never developed in that limited way. Today it is obvious to me that really fast and powerful runners, by my standards, at least, are not being developed, unless they add something extra to their training than running on the track, whether intermittently (interval training) or not.

Flat track training without added power will never produce the runners of the future capable of the customary efforts to be, such as the 3:50 mile (the 3:30 1,500 metres), the thirteen-minute three-mile, the twenty-seven-minute six-mile (equal to the 13:30 5,000 metres), and twenty-eight minutes, or less, for 10,000 metres.

It is also doubtful if the marathon runner of the future and his times will get the results of the future we can expect by running alone.

Strength can be greatly added to without increase in the bulk (size) of the muscles once the particular muscle has been developed to its proper size and function. The puny upper body, scraggy neck and shoulders, little or no pectorals, latissimus or abdominals, the stick-like arms we see on many distance runners, these are not particularly impressive to look upon even when the athlete has well-developed legs and lungs, and may (perhaps) run the mile in four minutes.

Beauty and strength: complete development transcends sheer goals and ambitions, not that I find weakly types do prevail, they don't. Some very lightly built types may look weak, but if they are very good athletes they will usually be found to be much stronger and wiry than may appear at first sight.

It is beyond dispute that most successful sprinters, 440-yard (400 metre) and many 880-yard (800 metre) types are good strong muscular types with good shoulders and arms.

However, no athlete can really claim to be strong who is unable to heave his body-weight overhead, or curl in loose style some 80 or 90 per cent of his body-weight. Those who can do no better than hoist 50 per cent of their body-weight overhead must be written off as amongst mankind's physical weaklings. Running alone is little likely to improve their sorry lot.

I divide the athletic year into three periods.

The first, and most important, is the Conditioning Period, which extends for at least six months of the year.

The second period is the Race Practice Period, and this approximates to about three months of the year.

The third period is devoted to the performance of that which we have been conditioned for, and have practised for, whatever it may be. All these periods, or phases, merge into each other.

Conditioning, then, for the athlete means he attempts by all those means I have mentioned to gain greater strength with which to attack his events in the forthcoming athletic season. He works and sweats to that end, and the cooler part of the year is the time for such endeavours and activities.

In Victoria (at Portsea) we condition from April through the winter to November. In this period we run much up sandhills wherever they are found, over sand dunes, on the 'heavy' part of the sandy beaches, occasionally we trudge up mountains; we work for two hours, at least, twice a week with the heaviest weights we can handle.

With what energy we may muster on occasion we go out for a long continuous run of upwards of twenty miles. This may happen once a month. And for a miler, three-miler type, we build up around 200 miles each month. We go into the surf occasionally during the winter as part of our toughening. We try to go to the snowfields once each winter. We use the horizontal and parallel bars as we can and do many 'sit-ups' and 'press-ups' at odd times. 'Conditioning' mentally and physically seems to go on almost continuously in our spare time away from work or studies.

During this period we may race occasionally across country for the sake of the interest only, never as a sport in itself. Therefore I insist that conditioning goes on on the morning of the race almost normally, and it was the custom, after the cross country race and a short spell, to run over the course a second time for added effort, training or conditioning! We consider a whole day, as we have in Australia, too much time to be wasted on merely one race, and that of no real importance, and providing, more often than not, only thirty minutes' hard effort, or five miles' running.

But we make it a practice, after the morning training which would not be exhausting on such a race day, to spend two hours in bed completely resting, and sleeping, if possible.

On the Sunday, after a hard race on the Saturday, we may miss the first training session, but usually the day's programme is carried through since the recovery should make this possible.

Cross country can never be more than a part of conditioning, since no true records are possible. The real champion wishes to excel, set records and compare himself accurately with his fellows. Only the track makes this possible. Further, only track events are completely international and occur in the great international competitions such as the Olympic Games.

We often train to exhaustion in this period. One has to break down to build up. Half-hearted efforts never accomplished much or achieved great objectives. But there must be reason in all things, and each one must find out to what degree the organism can be exhausted or punished without a deleterious effect.

If the effort has been extremely punishing, such as lifting maximum weights for two or three hours, or an hour's exhausting work on the sandhill, or a hard exhausting run up to twenty miles, it may take the organism a full forty-eight hours to recover, and severe weariness will indicate little or no training is possible until the organism has responded and recovered. We must be guided by our own feelings and experiences and remember both the body and the spirit can be broken down by overdoing the 'will' – or adhering wrongly to some imposed schedule.

A nice distinction must be made here as many athletes do not attain the success they otherwise may, simply because they exhaust the organism and do not permit sufficient time for recovery and the building-in of the added strength.

As we move into Race Practice we slowly taper off the Heavy Conditioning Work and move more into practising at the speeds and for the time we hope to race at. This means we shall visit the sandhill, or the beach, when we feel we may like some hard 'heavy' conditioning work – but broadly our work will now be devoted to two main factors, or efforts. We shall, fifty-fifty, do our running at the speeds we hope to race at and for as various distances as we are capable of, and also a lot of hard running for the racing time that is associated with our event or events.

Assume the 880 yards event. A lot of the running will be over various distances from, say, 100 yards to 600 yards at our full (hoped for, or pre-determined) race speed. Assume a training session of forty to sixty minutes is occupied in this manner, resting just as long between efforts as circumstances, not predetermination, determines. The next day the training session may be devoted to holding hard efforts for periods of time approximately 1:45 to two minutes. Thus the organism gets conditioned to moving freely at the essential speeds and holding hard efforts for the duration necessary.

However, there is much more to Race Practice than this. The athlete must condition his body to be able to vary pace, put in surges, 'take-off' and hold higher speeds for various distances, as well as practise making finishing runs from any part of the race as he may so determine.

We like to do this work over the parklands that are to be found in the city of Melbourne or upon the beautiful and hilly golf links that are located at Portsea. Some of this work is done on grass tracks; we never visit a cinder track for this purpose, or seldom use a stopwatch. It is remarkable how the organism can measure time, deliver speed and provide our best effort when it is required. To achieve this judgment the athlete has to be taught to trust his inner 'time recorder', which can measure out his speed and strength practically perfectly accurately if it but be trusted and responded to.

The stopwatch can never adequately train an athlete to pace judgment. Occasionally the athlete, or the coach, can use it to make checks as to progress, but even such checks and trials are often very discouraging. It is therefore better, when the athlete is a punishing and willing worker, to ignore time trials and the like completely.

By actual running an athlete soon finds out what is his top effort, say, for 880 yards, when he runs absolutely flat out for 600 yards! In his actual race he will need to be prepared to race another 280 yards at this flat out speed, as he probably will if he has also conditioned his body to hold very hard efforts for, say, 1:50.

Both the speed and the time factors become 'conditioned responses'. All the athlete needs is courage, the ability to suffer and the will to win.

These principles can be applied to all other track distances.

During this Race Practice period, Weight Resistance Work will be reduced to twenty-minute sessions two or three times a week, mostly heavy lifts – and whilst the work will be sweating hard as racing approaches care will be taken that it is not too exhausting.

Once racing starts, little or no conditioning training is done! We have built up to a strength-level and the object is now to exploit and demonstrate our strength and condition in fast racing.

Racing is best twice a week and between races just enough work, say twenty to thirty minutes, to keep the body and mind 'tuned up', fit and anxious to work!

Signs of staleness are (1) a loss of weight, (2) a marked disinclination to race, (3) a feeling of loss of strength.

However, this latter, the feeling of loss of strength, can be a temporary and psychological phenomenon and not necessarily an evidence of staleness when found without the other factors.

The cure for staleness is a complete let-up, if possible, from racing, for one or two weeks, visiting an entirely new environment such as the seaside – and forgetting athletics until the urge to run and race returns, as it will.

I think it should be apparent that, if any athlete in any sport is to perform better each season, two factors must be satisfied. He must acquire greater skill. He must become more powerful (stronger), both physically and mentally (spirit and knowledge).

Obviously, he can improve if only one factor is satisfied, but in a pastime such as running, if the simple movements are correct (perfect and natural), the second factor, power (strength), surely can be the only factor that can be expected to produce better (i.e. faster) times and performances.

That this is so has been my own personal experience. That it is so has made it possible for me to help, with a few simple suggestions, many athletes to faster times and better performances, not only in athletics but other sports such as cycling, and often when the orthodox and customary coaches and trainers have failed, signally, to produce any improvements in the performances of their charges.

CHAPTER 12

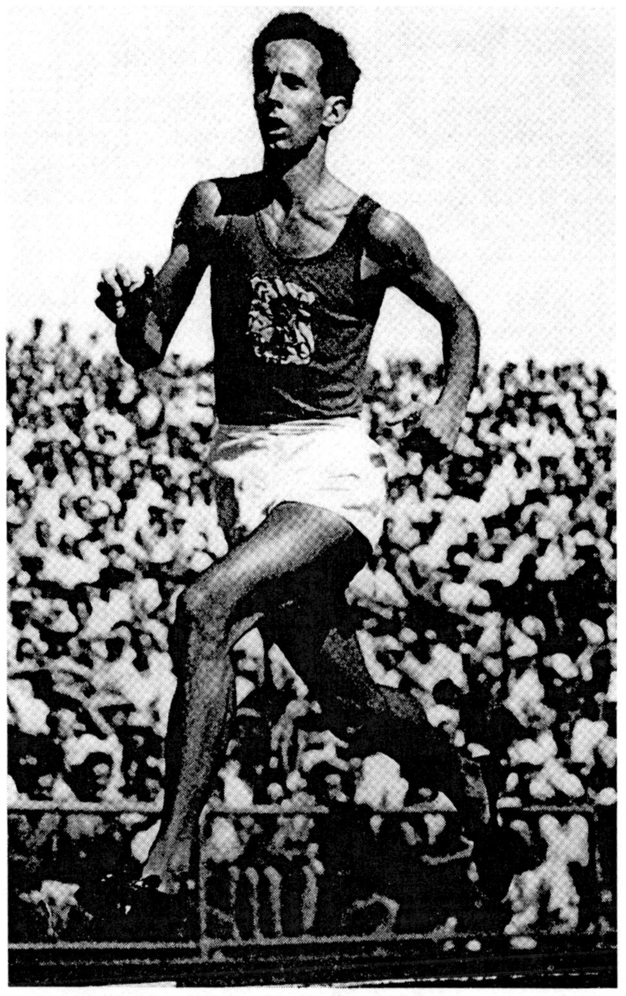

John Landy

John Landy setting a new Australian one mile record of 3:58.6. Caught in the middle of his stride, it is interesting to note the height of the bound, without which a long stride is well-nigh impossible. There must be no restriction on the movements. to me, it is wrong in any way to restrict the stride: to purposely cultivate a very low stride action, for instance. The object should be to get the strength to run freely with full, natural strides. Landy's pull-through arm-and-hand action can be seen and is good.

Dave Stephens

Dave Stephens, who followed Perry and set a new series of Australian distance records from the three mile up, culminating in a world record of 27:54 for six miles.

No athlete proved to be more easily teachable, not even Herb Elliott, and it was a common experience for Dave to run behind me almost to the end of his career, observing , imitating and acquiring the techniques and movements that I demonstrate and teach.

Geoff Warren

Geoff Warren – another great Australian distance runner who received his first lessons at Portsea. Warren ran, as did all the Portsea-trained athletes, with the body carriage and arm movements that distinguished these athletes, and caused considerable interest when it was first seen in England in 1952. Warren was, possibly, the first of my early athletes to hoist his body-weight overhead, using the barbell. It is their overall developed strength that causes them to run with a different style, rather than any taught technique, although the proper movements have to be taught in all cases.

CHAPTER 13

The Fundamental Movements

Mostly to do with the movements of the arms, hands and fingers and their relation to the trunk

In the beginning no effort should be made to assume postures. To tell an athlete to relax is to ask him to replace one set of tensions with another set. It is even worse when techniques of slack jaws and open hands are taught: the *sine qua non* of the weakly, always.

The athlete must be shown by personal demonstration what tension is; how to put it into his movements, and remove it.

Since so few understand the required movements, that is, what really constitutes good running, each and every well-meaning, or occupation-seeking, person who sets up as a coach or teacher will determine his own ideas of what is right and wrong. Mostly they are wrong.

Mostly, what does constitute good running, true relaxation, and absence of inhibiting tensions, can readily be seen when these things are demonstrated clearly and by opposites.

I have found, where I have had the opportunity of demonstrating, in a number of different countries, that I have no difficulty at all in demonstrating my points convincingly, although it is true that many who have supported and taught the traditional ideas have found they have incurred severe attacks of intellectual indigestion, and need to perform a mental somersault to accept my ideas. However, as results are self-evident to all, nothing can be said except, perhaps, as the old lady said when she saw the head of the giraffe above the fifteen-foot-high gate: 'I don't believe it!'

But the athletes themselves, no trouble at all! They see, and they accept, but they mostly find they cannot do it. Wrong education: wrong approaches: wrong traditions – not only athletically, but in regard to every single factor of their upbringing and education – have enslaved them, and free and full movement is mostly inhibited. Some never respond, even to a 30 per cent improvement; others gain as much as 50 per cent. By my standards and demonstrations I have not had one athlete, ever, who responded much above 70 per cent to what I would teach. Of the upper group undoubtedly Elliott, Stephens and an unknown, Kerry Cussen, would get highest marks. Cussen, by the way, starting from the weakest possible beginnings, was developed until only Elliott, with possibly one or two exceptions, exceeded him on the circuits at Portsea. He has never run seriously on the track because of personality trends that inhibit first-class public performances, a very common condition, I might add. He should have been world top-class, but his basic motivations fail him badly: he wilts and gives in. Some day, of course, he may attain to some reasonable success – if not in athletics, in something.

Indeed, the mental blockages to free physical expression, as well as to 'freed' mental approaches, are so serious that it is possible to say no athlete that I have associated with has ever been capable of delivering more than 80 per cent of the effort he could normally (by my standards) be expected to deliver, on a strength and conditioned basis, of his full powers. *All* are inhibited: *all* are fearful: all tend to hold back: *all* fail to believe *fully*: maybe this is because of being human, therefore governed to some extent by human frailties. Also due to youth. Absence of time to prove by experience of life and having, perforce, to believe, by education, in the mostly iniquitous sets of dogmas, that are openly and insidiously placed in the minds of our children and adolescents in the name of education, patriotism and religion.

So I teach by demonstration what constitutes tension and absence of tension and the means to achieve this most desirable end, no tensions whatever. These teachings incorporate the five basic arm and hand movements, so important to full and complete expression. In these movements when properly understood and carried out instinctively the hands open and close, clench and unclench, turn upon the axis of the wrist but *never* flap weakly on the wrist joint.

The strong are all strong-wristed; the unstable personality without true determination as to goals or directions will indicate his state by loose hands and weak wrists, grips and movements. One set of muscles alone, if we ignore the abdominals for the moment, can be considered tireless, to function without need of rest or relaxation, and these are the muscles which govern the firm forearm and, if we except axial movement, the rigid wrist, the clenching and unclenching fingers, which can remain and should remain clenched *all the time*, or with only momentary relaxing, in distance running; once the 'load is on' the race starts to hurt, and our determinations are called upon.

The normal and mostly used arm movement is the low arm carriage. In this the hand moves from a side position corresponding to the side seam of the running 'knicks' or shorts. The arm with an elbow that *moves* on its hinges, and the arm partly bent, throws upwards, forwards and partly across the body. The thumb rests lightly on the forefinger or is in contact somewhere.

The same movement, in its fullest and most exaggerated form, is the full sprint action. Care should be taken that the hands do not pass much or any distance behind the side centre line, and when vigorously thrown forwards do not cross, but *reach* an imaginary centre line projected outwards from the centre of the body. This means that the hands move to a position in full sprinting that approximates to mouth level and directly in front of the mouth but, almost, full arm's-length out in front.

It is a mistake for the arms to work closely across the chest, although such an arm position, by the shortened stroke due to the bent arm and power being delivered more readily by this close and compact movement, does suggest itself as a means of developing speed. But the movement is constrictive, tends to tensions and is the opposite of 'free and full-flowing'.

The next important arm position, used by Emil Zatopek, is the 'rest' or 'crucified' position. The whole organism is partly rested whilst it runs on the legs, by holding the arms high up and close to the chest, with the palms turned upwards and the fingers open, or relaxed.

A few strides taken in this way in distance running rests the athlete and permits him to resume the drives and pressures essential to supreme efforts.

Then there is the use of the arms by thrusting them violently downwards, a movement which tends to force the body up off the ground in readiness to running 'over it', rather than 'upon it'.

With this movement, which also incorporates the 'give away' or rejection of the task, is the 'acceptance' or 'gather in'. The arms are thrown down and out, the hands open, palms down, but immediately the hands turn palm upwards the fingers close and the arms raise the hands high up to breast level. These two movements have great psychological value as well as preparing the physical body to run.

The last of the important fundamental movements, and used extensively by both Elliott and Thomas (both world records), is the 'throw' or 'crawl' movement. The arms throw the hands outwards and downwards, the hands tending to make an elongated downward throw or thrust rather than the customary upward one. It is not unlike the primary swimming movement used in dog-paddling or a child crawling. This movement used in the 'warm-up' is also used when tired and a surge is instituted. With both Elliott and Thomas it is an integral part of their movements at all times. With its use the leg carriage remains low and the stride seems to reach out without undue strain, effort or apparent over-striding.

In all these movements the body tends to rise and fall with the rise and fall of the diaphragm as the respiration becomes deep and full. The arms also bend to follow oscillating curves. Above all the elbows move. Nothing inhibits good movements and shoulder steadiness more than locked or immovable elbows – perhaps the most common, as it is also one of the most serious of the defects seen in runners.

Every muscle works, even the facials, and *every* hinge (joint) moves, especially the elbows.

According to my ideas, all running *starts* with the thumbs and *ends* in the feet. No effort is made to control the foot landing, yet this is light and almost noiseless. Pounding is evidence of absence of true lift – and the *over*-use of power (strength) rather than its more effective use by skilled technique.

The head moves on the shoulders as if on a ball and socket, free but without wobble. It turns easily as we run to observe round about us, as is essential if we are to watch our competitors!

The chest 'feels' flattened: never protruded as in the 'attention' position – the abdomen is held back and the pelvis observed (if we could see it) to be up-tilted slightly.

In perfect running there is no pronounced knee lift or kick-up at the back. The feet follow a track that is best thought of as an elongated ellipse like the caterpillar track of a vehicle, not the round, wheel-like circular motion acceptable as normal a few years back.

However, it is the strength of the upper body that properly and in balanced development ensures the correct postures and alignments; and the legs and feet follow on normally and naturally. No effort must be made to run by controlled or taught leg movements. They will be correct, if all else is correct, therefore can be ignored, in themselves. Correct body alignment is recognized when the runner can see his knees lifting in front of him, without moving his head, only looking down, and when his eyes are raised and level he sees an artificial horizon.

He sees, without conscious looking, each footfall, and should not lose or relinquish this good running form as he tires and approaches the finish. An almost universal evidence of poor coaching and finishing technique is the throwing back of the head, the eyes looking skywards, the chest protruding, the arms waving wildly, all good running form being lost.

It can be argued that I have repeated some of the points here which I stressed in Chapter 6. There is no harm in repetition to bring home a point here and there.

Chapter 14

Summed up: How can it be done? What is the 'Way'? What path, philosophy, code or training schedule must you follow? The 'measure -rod' for success

1. To be born with above average ability but not necessarily outstanding ability.
2. You need an intelligence suitable for the tasks ahead of you. This needs to be of a high order. But I make a distinction between intelligence (wisdom) and cleverness which may be only cunning and memory. It is far more important that you have a good I.Q. than you can merely pass exams. If you 'feel' you have above average ability, both physically and mentally, that is enough.
3. You need a persistence factor that does not easily give in – give up when not successful; that can train on, struggle on, when things look hopeless, black.
4. You need to be one of those whose spirits rise and you feel 'good' when things are tough in adversity; one who is a 'tiger for punishment'; does not talk about 'sacrifices'; and sees, mostly, the goals to be attained to.
5. You need to be one who finds working hard for what they want normal; is surprised when they find others expect short cuts, ease of accomplishment.

6. Who believe that they could do 'it' – or something, and feel confirmed and pleased when they find their 'beliefs' can come true; that someone else may, surprisingly as it seems, believe so, too.
7. You are one who will:
   (a) Change your job, environment, country even, if it seems right to do so, to achieve your ends (not only athletic ends).
   (b) Have a natural, inherent attitude to be attracted, seek or find the 'best', whether it be in coaches, music, places or persons.

The 'Measure–rod' for Success

If you are destined to 'high honours' by successes, you will find you are, or have started already, conforming to the 'blueprint for success' as laid down in this book. You are 'already on the way' doing many of the things suggested; that the ideas 'confirm' rather than upset your pre-conceived ideas of things.

Therefore you will take readily and easily to the ideas suggested in this book; you will find yourself lifting heavy weights, or wanting to; running up hills hard, or doing so once the idea has been suggested to you. In a word, being what the boys dubbed themselves, suggestively, 'Cerutty-men', since we must have terms and ideas to express our thoughts and aspirations. We are not a society or club; we have no rules, no binding promises, no slavish loyalties, but we do find we are of the gang of good fellows who feel common bonds with one another, who aspire to greatness rather than worship it – who, whilst they feel co-operative, feel, nevertheless, intensely competitive, not inclined to stand aside for any man!

In the beginning you may have your heroes, those who seem miraculous in their doings, far above your wildest dreams, but it is not long before you also realize you are one of the 'accepted' in the great caravan who march steadily to their goals, that the sky is their limit, nothing is impossible, and in the simple words of a much-respected Ceylon friend of mine, D. Ponambalam, Esq., 'It can be done!'

In the beginning you must be *strong*, inordinately strong, not necessarily muscularly big but far above average – tough, resistant, powerful, muscularly superior. Or make yourself strong.

What parts must be strong? The heart must be large and powerful, the, lung capacity good, the chest-box big – that is, wide, deep and thick through. Too many judge the physique by 'wide' shoulders. Often the distance from the neck to the navel is short, the distance through from the front to the back poor. All these things can be tested, checked up on. It is the 'cubical content' of your chest-box in relation to your total size and weight that is important, not that you are wide across the shoulders, or have a 'peg-top' physique.

Actually the strongest types tend to be parallel-sided, not noticeably wide across the shoulders, but noticeably big and powerful around the waist and abdominals. This is seen in studies of men of the eminence in the physical culture and strength world of Sandow and Hackenschmidt.

So, we set out to become inordinately strong. This is done by working against resistance – sand, hills, water, snow for the legs, body-weight through the medium of ropes and other gym apparatus, and barbells for the trunk. What exercises do I favour? Or, if you prefer it, upon what 'system' or exercises was Elliott developed? Here it is:

In the beginning Elliott came to me strong. His early life, his love of hard work, rowing at school, all developed him above average. I merely carried the work further. He was immediately put to lifting the heaviest weights he was capable of. We have ample barbells; a horizontal bar and gym provide other apparatus. Herb took to it all like a duck to water, as all the 'boys' do. He would do press ups, leg lifts, bar chins, sit ups as he felt impelled; nothing rigidly laid down, mostly as the fit takes us – although the rule is, *some* hard exercise, daily.

I give an outline in the next chapter.

Chapter 15

Resistance exercises using the body: the barbell and the dumbbell as added resistance

In the work with weights, I have simplified the exercises; others can be added with advantage, but the fundamental exercises I like myself are as follows:

(N.B. I am aware that there is some repetition here with Chapter 11, but I want to get these points home to you.)

1. The snatch. To warm-up.
2. The rowing motion. For arms, shoulders and abdominals.
3. The press. For pushing muscles, standing (military), bench press or best of all with heavy dumbbells, exercising each arm alternately.
4. Curls. Front and reverse.
5. The dead-lift. With erect, straight back.
6. One-handed swings.

The boys are also fond of pull-downs where the apparatus is available.

A brief description of each of these varied exercises may be helpful. We shall commence with the exercises using the body as the resistance weight to be moved.

The Press-up.

The athlete lies face downwards and moves his body off the

floor or earth by straightening his arms. When the exercise is completed the body is supported by the arms and rests on three-point suspension, the arms, the toes, the body being rigid. Six to sixty times. Exercises shoulders and arms.

Leg lifts.

Athlete lies prostrate on back, lifts legs keeping hands by side palms down until toes touch floor behind head. Six to sixty times. Good for abdominals and flexibility.

Chinning the bar. The athlete seizes any bar, bough of tree, door lintel, lets the body hang supine and then pulls it to chin level with the bar or just above it. Six to twenty, mostly arms and fingers.

Sit ups.

The athlete lies prone on back, feet under ledge of furniture, bar of barbell or strap on wall; hands are placed behind head, and body is raised until head assumes a position between knees. The knees can bend and to make the exercise more vigorous weights from barbell can be held behind the head and/or the exercise done on an inclined board, the feet being as much as three feet above floor level. Six to one hundred movements depending upon whether the exercise is done in the simplest and easiest or hardest forms. Very good for the abdominals especially.

Some flexibility exercises may be done with advantage such as toe-touching – opposite hand to opposite toes, standing or sitting with legs apart, and similar. But it must be understood that exercises, like the cycling exercise – athlete lying on back, buttocks supported by hands and legs moving as if cycling – do little to contribute to increased strength, and flexibility exercises in general will do little for any athlete with the possible exception of jumpers, vaulters and hurdlers.

Even with them, more than five minutes daily on such exercises is time that could be more usefully used.

So to the work with heavy resistance.

It needs to be understood that I am one who holds certain and definite opinions upon the use of heavy resistance. They are:

1. No one can become *really* strong except by the use of heavy resistances.
2. Few repetitions with very heavy weights, *not* many repetitions with relatively light weights.
3. There is little to be gained by doing unusual exercises, freakish exercises or jumping movements with light weights.
4. I do not believe in deep knee-bends or full squats with heavy weights for athletes. They will make the legs powerful, it is true, but enlarge the thigh muscles abnormally and do not seem to make for added running speeds and have adversely affected the knees of some athletes. For the legs I much prefer using the body as resistance, hard and repetitive efforts up steep sandhills, any hills, many flights of stairs, etc. It is not so important that the legs be made unusually or abnormally strong as is required by the stunt strong man, but that all the organism be made strong, including the heart. Hard resistance running will do this, better and simply. It is the upper body, abdominals and back muscles that are usually deficient in power in athletes, and the exercises are to strengthen them, in particular.

WEIGHT RESISTANCE EXERCISES

The snatch, to warm up.

A weight is placed on the barbell that makes it reasonably easy to lift the barbell from its position on the floor to a position at arms'-length overhead in one upward heave-and-throw movement. Ten repetitions carried out once only is sufficient. A weight about one-fourth or one-third of the athlete's body-weight is sufficient. The exercise is meant merely to loosen up and prepare us for the harder and more vigorous exercises to come.

The rowing motion

Weight is placed on the barbell about 50 per cent of body-weight or alternatively what can be moved six times without extreme effort, but ten times only with extreme effort.

For a beginner this latter direction will be found to be approximately 50 per cent body-weight or even as low as 30 per cent.

The legs kept straight, and feet planted firmly on floor, the body is bent over until approximately parallel with floor, and weight is lifted clear of the floor and then the arms draw the weight close to the body in a somewhat circular movement, using the arms as in rowing, hence the name. Six to ten efforts.

When ten can be done without resorting to extreme effort, add more weight and drop the repetitions to six again. After a short rest, repeat the six to ten repetitions three times, making a total of eighteen to thirty movements. The arms are benefited, the legs by virtue of the 'held' tension whilst the exercise is in progress, and the abdominals especially by virtue of held tension.

NOTE: There seems to be some evidence that muscle groups that are held, or would be held, in Nature, in continued tension, seem to be considerably strengthened by being submitted to this continued tension even more than being flexed and released, that is moved, in slow rhythmic movements even with very heavy resistances. Especially is this true of the abdominal and back groups – together with the muscles situated in the forearm and those which move and tension the fingers, causing them to close and remain clenched, as they should.

The modern athletic concept of relaxation through unclenched fists is what actually causes tensions, not only in the fingers and arms but all over the trunk and the neck muscles in particular.

The press

A heavy barbell or preferably a dumbbell is hoisted into position resting on the upper chest and is pushed overhead until held at full arms' length overhead, letting it return to the chest position. If this exercise can be executed ten times consistently without pause, then the weight used should be increased until six is a reasonably hard effort – ten almost impossible.

When it is found ten 'reps' can be done consistently, add another two and a half pounds to the dumbbell and revert to six repetitions; a total of three sets of six to ten. Exercise the weaker arm last and even if unable to complete the 'reps' with this weaker arm, do so after a brief rest.

Curls

Front and reverse. One of the most important exercises for runners who are usually weak in the arms. The barbell or dumbbell (for use of each arm alternately) hangs at full arms' length and is brought up to upper chest level by flexing the biceps. For an athlete's purposes this exercise should be done in the method known as 'cheating'.

In this, all of the upper body is used, not kept immobile as in the classic method of the weight-lifter. After six to ten repetitions are done with the barbell held with the palms uppermost, have a slight rest.

Six to ten reps are done with the reverse grip, that is with the palms downwards. Three sets of six to ten 'reps' in each of the two grips, thirty-six to sixty movements in all, make for adequate exercise in this essential development of the arms and upper body.

The dead-lift

CHAPTER 15

If there is one part of the anatomy that seems to indicate the general inadequacy and decadence of the modern male it is the weakness of the back and abdominals.

No man who lifts heavy weights consistently can suffer from this 'masculine malady' with all its consequent psychological and physiological repercussions, probably the most widespread and serious civilized man is the victim of.

A heavy barbell is placed on the ground in front of the 'patient'. He lowers himself until his buttocks are as close to the ground as is essential to reach the bar. His back is kept as erect and straight as possible and he hoists the weight off the ground or floor by thrusting with his legs until he is erect and the bar hangs from the extended arms.

When erect he continues the movement by pulling the shoulders back until the shoulder blades touch. He lowers the weight by keeping as erect as possible but letting the legs fold under him. On no account should he bend over the bar with straight legs and a bowed back parallel with the ground. There is always a liability of pulling back muscles, strains and displaced organs even.

Also, a weight commencing at three-quarters of bodyweight, or what can be lifted twenty times with full effort, will be the correct weight to handle. Such a weight lifted ten times in sets of three is sufficient for the needs of athletes, as distinct, perhaps, from those aiming to be 'strong men' or specialists in dead-lifting.

However, the exercise can be repeated as much as one wishes, I myself having lifted some seventy thousand foot-pounds in a day's workout, but whether the training is done with a lot of repetitions or as occasionally may be justified, one or more lifts with the maximum weight one can hoist off the ground – the athlete should be alert to the possibility of groin strains, and desist the moment a feeling of strain appears in the region of the lower abdomen on either side.

Nevertheless, a fear of a possible strain should not prevent really hard, long and consistent exercising with heavy weights – it is sufficient if one is alert to the feelings of real strain, not imaginary ones which stop lesser people whatever may be the exercise they indulge in. One can feel the 'drawing down' of the long muscles of the abdomen before strain is really possible.

Even if a strain does eventuate there is rarely a rupture. I have never heard of a rupture in anyone who exercises consistently or intelligently, and the strain usually clears up in a few weeks, even if a serious one. It is wise to abandon the dead-lift for the time being if there is a strain, but it is O.K. to resume when the feeling of strain or soreness disappears.

The one-handed swings

A dumb-bell is loaded to a weight that can be swung from between the legs to a position over the head with a straight arm. In the beginning difficulty with balance may be experienced but in no time the athlete should be swinging from one-third to one-half body-weight to the usual formula: six to ten 'reps' each arm without rest between change-over, and adding more weight when ten can be accomplished with each arm, as routine.

In this exercise every muscle of the legs and trunk can be felt playing its part, and should be moved vigorously. No single exercise is more conducive to making it normal for the athlete to move with full mobility of the arms and trunk; to feel, as he runs, the rise and fall of the body, the rise and fall of the diaphragm and the full and effective delivery of power of every part of his musculature.

What happens to many athletes is the immobility of the upper body, hampering them in full inhalations and exhalations of the lungs, as well as inhibiting full power efforts. It is not unusual for an athlete who can quickly acquire this full use of himself to find that his performances over distances such as the 440 yards, 880 yards and one mile especially, have improved by two, four and up to ten seconds respectively, merely by the complete uninhibited movements of his diaphragm and trunk musculature generally.

Naturally this will not apply to a runner who already runs the 440 in 47, the 880 in 1:48 and the mile in four minutes, but it easily can in the athlete, otherwise well trained and strong, who finds difficulty in *reaching* the times I quote.

A fuller, freer, uninhibited (zombie-like) use of himself is often *his* answer.

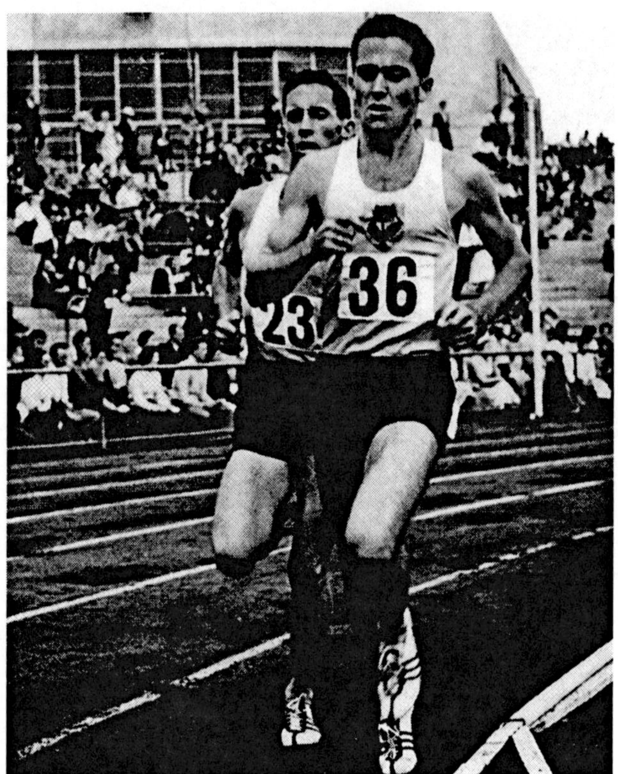

Lawrence and Thomas

Allan Lawrence running with Albert Thomas. At first Lawrence, who was many years senior to Thomas, and at one time supreme in Australia as a six-miler, defeated Thomas with regular consistency. But this was soon to pass. All 'Cerutty-trained' athletes are taught to be front runners. If they have the fundamental ability to see it out, this policy makes for real success on the highest levels.

Note the head, gaze, arm positions and finger positions. No strain, unbalance or shoulder sway is evident. In this race, which Thomas won early in 1957 in the time of 13:37.6, very close to the then world record, the quality of the effort can be seen in the expressions of both these Australians.

Albert Thomas

Competing with other Portsea athletes, Elliott and Wilson, a new 4 x 1 mile relay word record was run. Note the low arm carriage favoured by Portsea-trained athletes; the erect body carriage with only slight forward lean; the good head position; the lightly landed foot eased down to the track by the well-held body that has not slumped at all as the body commences to pass over the foot.

This is only possible when the body is strong and well developed muscularly. Note the absence of spectators, indicative of the interest or lack of it, in athletics in Australia, except on rare occasions.

Chapter 16

Off-season training: the fundamentals of basic conditioning: with special reference to sprinters

If one would succeed, on the highest levels, in the future I think it is evident we have to do something, or do a little more, than was thought sufficient, or effective, in the past. In particular, perhaps that applies more to sprinters and athletes who wish to succeed in a world-class way up to 800 metres and the miles more than distance men.

First-class distance men, three miles, six miles and marathon, always did do plenty of work all the year round. But to this day it has not been considered advantageous for a dash man - a sprinter who confined his efforts to 100 yards (or metres) to 220 yards (or 200 metres) - to be able to run up to five miles efficiently. Indeed it is the general assumption that to do so is to ruin any potential he may have of being a first-class sprinter. The reverse is the truth, but there are contributory factors that have to be taken cognizance of.

These factors are: the dash, or sprint athlete, who attempts to run distance with his (usual) artificial gait (when his speed is considerably reduced); that is, he usually attempts to run slowly with a long stride, a bounding gait, his legs and feet tensed to a ball-of-foot landing and arms full of tension. He is usually so tensed and tied up that he is labouring painfully, or actually brought to a standstill before he has covered a mile in as slow a time as 4:30. Often he cannot achieve a five-minute mile, so tensed and strained are his movements. This should not, and need not, be so.

But it *is* proof that most sprinters have little idea how to run slowly, just as natural and important a thing as running fast; nor do their coaches have the necessary knowledge to help them. So has grown up the idea that a distance run, an ability to run a fast mile, or a reasonable five-mile or ten-mile, is inimical to the interests of the sprinter. This is not true.

It is true that if a man wishes to be a first-class sprinter he must *specialize* in fast running, but this need not mean the total absence of ability to run further and to do it efficiently and in a workmanlike manner. But it does suggest, as I have found, that the sprinter has to be taught how to run at slower paces than his customary flat-out bursts, and that when he is so taught, and then conditions himself by more running at steady paces, *his ability to run fast increases.* By attempting to run in his normal manner he can easily, and usually does, impair his natural ability to run fast. This is the predicament that faces most dash men, and the suggested solution in a book is not necessarily an easy solution in practice.

True running at easy paces involves a low foot carriage, a heel landing, no knee-lift or kick-up, and arms hanging almost straight, kicking forwards and slightly across. No attempt is made to stride out. The forefingers lightly pinch on to the thumbs.

Such movements in no way impair a sprinter's ability to run fast. When correctly done, the reverse is the case, the dash man will run faster because he is practising in such slow running, true posture, running movements and relaxation. To me, those who drop as low as the nine-second 100 yards (ten-second 100 metres) or lower, as we shall find in the future, will certainly be those who can run at least up to five miles, if need be, in the proper running movements as I have outlined them. It is true that to do so will not necessarily produce a nine-second 'hundred' man - there are other factors, obviously - but it will be part of the equipment of the fast men of the future. I hold if you cannot do it *perfectly slowly*, the athlete is little likely to do it perfectly fast; to me it is essential that the athlete must be drilled and supervised to do his work at slow speeds, first, before we can expect the ultimates in the full effort.

I also hold, if he cannot come out of the blocks perfectly poised and balanced in slow motion, a fast getaway is likely to be covering up defects that he may otherwise eliminate by mastering full control of his organism at *all* paces.

When this is acquired, as I visualize it, the dash man of the future will be able to produce at will a series of accelerating bursts or surges. It is known that, for perhaps thirty yards, a sprinter can run very fast; if he could produce his top speed for the full 100 yards, the sub-nine-second would now be an accomplished fact.

I feel that the athlete can be trained to run in a series of pulses, waves, or surges that will attain this very desirable end: a top pace maintained for every yard of the distance even to a slight acceleration for the whole of the distance. I concede it will be difficult to maintain such an acceleration beyond the 100 yards or we would find we were running the 220 yards (200 metres) in times approximating to eighteen seconds. I hardly expect this although I believe coaches will solve the problem of technique and training that will result in sub-twenty-second 220 yards becoming reasonably commonplace. And so on up the scale of distances.

These improvements will come from the appreciation of, and practise of; pulse or wave running. Everything pulses in Nature; there is ebb and flow, a wave system is found in all or most things; nothing is static; nothing fixed or permanent; nothing without oscillation of some kind, yet athletes run as if their energy poured out in a steady stream. Stereotyped fixed beats or paces instead of fluctuating movements, no matter how tenuous. Running is movement, but *variety in those move-*

ments is the essence of it. Enough research and experimentation has been done to prove the possibility of such ideas. Just how much of Elliott's superiority is due to his ability to surge, to rest and run without losing speed, indeed, accelerating apparently effortlessly, how much is due to such techniques, first taught but now entirely instinctive, one can only guess at. But I do suggest there is much room for test and trial, research and experiment, by those capable of doing this much needed work and with suitable athletes to work upon.

So my sprinter of the future would be taught how to run slowly, each movement would be isolated and analysed. He would be taught the techniques that would result in the complete control of his musculature and movements, and would be able to accelerate at will. Being strengthened, his stride would be longer but his tempo, at least, maintained. It is amazing what even an increase in the stride of only three inches will do when the power is available to maintain the same tempo. In 100 yards it can mean an improvement of 0.3 of a second, an improvement sufficient, at the present time, to bring the record down to a flat nine seconds or possibly a tenth under the nine seconds, viz. 8.9 seconds! If we add an accelerating factor of only 0.01 we find we are, with certainty, below nine seconds for the hundred. I am surprised it is not already accomplished.

Chapter 17

Gymnastics and extra exercise are a must.

It is not sufficient, in my opinion, that an athlete who would aim at world-class standards should confine his activities to running training and upper body development.

I feel that there is a positive need for the practise of other activities. These are undertaken to gain better balance, resilience, flexibility, and an all-over, all-round development.

For this reason we indulge in a reasonable amount of swimming. My athletes will ride bicycles for exercise to school or work if they find it advantageous: certainly they are not forbidden these activities. All is grist that comes to our mill. But I am emphatic that if we wish to excel at running we shall do much more running than cycling or swimming. Everything must be kept in proper proportion: seen in correct perspective. What is this proportion or perspective?

In Australia, the climate for six months of the year is admirably suited to swimming: so we swim, or bathe, in the sea most days. If we have had a 'teaching' period on the track, when we all run very intensively, we will go to the beaches and spend an hour bathing, swimming, diving and sun-bathing. Then home for lunch and the siesta.

Or we train on the sand dunes, or along the beaches, to finish off with a ten to twenty minutes surfing: a very exhilarating pastime, and indulged in through the winter, but for shorter periods.

I also recommend the occasional use of the gymnasium apparatus, such as the horizontal and parallel bars, roman rings, and the horse. All such equipment makes for dexterity, strength and zest. One day's training session each week might well be devoted to such activities. Climbing the rope is a very good exercise for any athlete.

Tumbling, somersaulting, hand-balancing and similar feats, all contribute, in my opinion, to the well-being and fitness, both mental and physical, of the athlete. In a properly organized regime a part of the time of every athlete would be planned and devoted to these 'extra' activities: as much as four hours per week.

Occasional mountain-walking trips, rock-climbing expeditions, or just long walks or runs, all build up stamina and strength under 'play' conditions and do much to vary the tedium of regular athletic training. As long as a reasonable mileage is covered each month, dictated by the event trained for, and the training be hard and intensive, much good can come from these other activities that are more extensive in their nature.

Of course, conditions, environmental and economic, probably make it impossible for 90 per cent of athletes to live a life, or enjoy a regime, that could be construed to provide 100 per cent results. However, the athletes who gather round me, never more than ten or twenty at any one time, and subjected to all the disabilities inherent in our economic system as it impresses itself on young students and workers, all strive to enjoy some walks in the mountains: some long runs of twenty or thirty miles: some gymnastics, etc., even if the opportunities are very infrequent, say, only twice a year for mountain-walking weekends, or long runs.

Nevertheless, such activities seem to produce results above and out of proportion in good results, in zest, stamina and strength, to the incidence of their enjoyment.

It is also to be noted that many of the world's greatest runners also achieved much ability in other pastimes such as skiing, or boxing, or activities usually not associated with them. Nevertheless, when all is said and done, if one wants to excel as a runner, it is running that must be mostly practised, concentrated upon, and in the hours devoted to exercise the ratio for middle-distance athletes could be around 60:40, the sixty, of course, being purely running practice. As we go up the scale to the marathon, the time as applied to exercise might well be 80:20. With the sprinter he could well find the ratio as low as 30:70, quite a big part of his exercise time being devoted in the off-season to other pastimes, such as tumbling, gymnastics, basketball or similar sporting activities. Table tennis may prove satisfactory.

My own instincts and activities have been along these lines since I became re-interested in athleticism. In one period of five years I not only ran approximately 10,000 miles, but walked many thousands in long 'hikes' of fifty to five hundred miles in our mountain system; but also regularly practised weight-lifting, head and hand-stands, and some horizontal bar work.

I find that the normal instincts of the younger athletes are all in the same direction. Even if these activities did not assist the development of the athlete, I would be favourable to them as a part of the pattern of living a complete and interesting life.

All natural activities must contribute to the general wellbeing of the athlete. His nature will tend to indicate his individual needs. Those destined for the 'top' will tend to make few mistakes: their selectivity will be better: They will 'waste' little time or effort. All they do will contribute more efficiently to their development: to the achieving of their goals. Experience, and an instinct for the best, will be their best teacher. The coach can but watch over: suggest: never dictate. Especially without adequate and convincing reasons.

Athletics seems to be the one activity in which authoritarianism fails, at least more than in most fields.

Chapter 18

The proper and efficient use of the self: the importance of understanding our own body and its components, and acquiring the ability to move it in every way: posture and running movement that make for the efficiency aimed at

Most athletes, like most people, can be likened to the animal that seeks to gain its ends, but without the proper use of its intelligence. A chained dog, endeavouring to reach meat that is out of its reach, will strive and tug at its chain, and completely ignore a crooked stick, which, even held in its mouth, could be expected to easily drag the food within reach.

So it is with most athletes. In concentrating upon their 'ends' they almost completely ignore a study of the means whereby they can move their organism to better advantage so that they run faster, further, easier.

Indeed, it is almost universally desired to discover the 'schedule' that the successful athlete has trained to, as if the copying of any schedule could be expected to produce the same result for another athlete irrespective of place, age, type, disposition, initial strength, initial ability and other factors.

It is so evident to me that it is useless to train long and seriously until a tyro has mastered the elements of correct movement as I teach it, that little running is done in the initial stages. Every effort is made to acquire the use of the self: to be able to put tension into the musculature, and to remove it, at will: consciously and with full control. Otherwise it seems useless to me to talk about relaxation.

The proper use of the self implies the proper movement of the trunk and the understanding of the effect of the various movements of the upper body upon the legs and feet: the footfall and landing, as well as the length of stride, the kick-up and other movements.

The athlete learns what is bad about shoulder sway, why it is there, how to bring it in, how to remove it at will. What arm movements cause it and what proper arm movements remove this, probably, worst fault in modern running.

How the shoulders, drawn or pulled back, cause side instead of cross-body movements of the arms. That when the shoulders are allowed to fall freely forward the arms swing as I have described elsewhere, and which is found in all first-class performers.

It is from the control of the musculature, from much time put into mastering this control, that, again, in my opinion, the superlative times of the future can be expected to result.

With this use it is easy to demonstrate, at easy paces, a natural stride of up to three metres, or three yards. And experiments have shown me that athletes not trained to such control and use of the abdominals find great difficulty in striding at an easy pace up to such distances as three yards or metres. Indeed, in most cases, without introducing an obvious jump, such a stride length is impossible for them.

The ability to stride in this way with effortless ease can be taught, and is reasonably easily mastered by any athlete. I do not go so far as to say an athlete can maintain it, or if he could that it would necessarily be an advantage But it certainly is a part of our technique to be able to quicken the tempo at will: to lengthen the stride at will: to surge at will: and to understand the various bodily movements, without which such variations are often outside the experience of many athletes. These athletes find that it is not necessarily exhaustion that makes it impossible to follow Elliott when he surges away from them, or some other fast-finishing athlete passes them. Not at top speed themselves they find the greatest difficulty in accelerating. They may go a little faster, but often suffer the chagrin of being beaten by another athlete who is able to do things such as accelerating at will, whilst they, the beaten athletes, finish less exhausted, but remark that they could not go any faster.

I am not speaking of flat-out sprint running, but even in that, ability, and the means to accelerate at will, must be sought. This ability arises out of an understanding of the use of the self: that consciousness, in the learning stages, of the dropping of the arms and the body: the slight forward drop without which sudden acceleration is impossible.

The correct use of the self also implies the well-sustained rise and fall of the diaphragm, and with it the rise and fall of the body, so that the head follows a varying height line. The arms weave, thrust and pull with a sinuous motion. They, also, rise and fall in their carriage-height according to the demands being made upon the whole running organism.

These cyclic wave motions are not necessarily very obvious, but the athlete must have them: must be conscious of them: able to vary and use them at will.

Even the forward progression should be in a series of forward-moving waves or cycle beats. Not necessarily obvious, but there all the same. Everything in Nature conforms to a pulse or rhythm, to wave motions, surges and rest periods. The athlete must seek the means to use these things, to feel them in his own experience, if he would achieve the ends that lead to superlative performance. All stereotyped, zombie-like movements must be replaced by an intelligent use and understanding of the means whereby faster times will be run – as they will.

APPENDIX I

The chief races in Herb Elliott's running career

AS A SCHOOLBOY:

Age 15 years

	At Perth: Western Australia	880 yards	I:58.2
	1 mile	4:30.8	

Age 16 years

6.11.54	At Perth: State Schoolboy Championships	1 mile	4:25.6
3.1.55	At Perth: Inter–schools Championships	1 mile	4:26.8
5.2.55	At Adelaide, South Australia: Junior (under 19 years) Championships	880 yards	1:55.7
7.2.55	Same meet, two days later	1 mile	4:20.8

Age 17 years

17.9.55	At Perth: School Championship	1 mile	4:22
29.10.55	At Perth: Schoolboy Championships	1 mile	4:20.4

Age 18 years

26.12.56	At Frankston, Victoria: Running from Scratch in a handicap as a trial. (Did not win)	880 yards	1:54
12.1.57	At Melbourne: V.A.A.A. Inter–Club Competitions (World junior record)	1 mile	4:06
19.1.57	At Melbourne: Inter–Club Competitions	880 yards	1 :53.7
26.1.57	At Melbourne: Victorian Championships	1 mile	4:06
28.1.57	ditto	880 yards	1:50.8

9.2.57	At Adelaide: South Australia Junior Championships	1 mile	4:06.2
14.2.57	At Melbourne: Evening Meet (World junior record)	2 miles	9:01
16.2.57	At Sydney: NSW Championships (a very strong wind blowing)	1 mile	4:06.4
20.2.57	At Box Hill: Evening Club Meet. Rough track (New World junior record)	1 mile	4:04.4
23.2.57	Melbourne: Inter–Club Meet	3 miles	14:02.4

(In this race Elliott ignored the opposition and ran merely to set a new Australian 3,000 metres junior record – a record which he accomplished in 8:45.6. He then continued in the race and ran second to Geoff Warren, at the full three-mile distance, recording a new World junior record for that distance).

On his birthday, February 25th, Elliott held all the Australian Junior Records for the 800 metres, 880 yards, 1,500 metres, 1 mile, 3,000 metres, two miles and three miles. In addition Elliott had recorded the best times ever run in the world by a youth of eighteen years for one mile, two miles and three miles.

Age 19 years

9.3.57	At Melbourne: Australian Championships	1 mile	4:00.4
11.3.57	ditto	880 yards (800 metres)	1:49.3 (1:48.6)
	(The fastest ever by an Australian)		
13.10.57	At Mornington: A country meet to aid a charity	3 miles	14:18
22.10.57	At Hamilton: a country town (An exhibition race by Cerutty athletes)	3/4 mile	3:00.5
18.1.58	At Melbourne: Inter–Club Meet	880 yards	1:51.8
25.1.58	ditto	1 mile	3:59.9
30.1.58	ditto. Evening Meet	1 mile	3:58.7
15.2.58	At Perth: Western Australia. Championships	1 mile	3:59.6
26.2.58	At Perth: ditto	880 yards	1:49.5

Age 20 years

9.3.58	At Toowoomba: Queensland	1,000 metres	2:21

15.3.58	At Brisbane: Australian Championships	1 mile	4:08.8
17.3.58	ditto	880 yards	1:49.4

In U.S.A.

16.5.58	At Los Angeles	1 mile	3:57.8
	(American Record and the second fastest mile then on record)		
31.5.58	At Modesto	1 mile	4:02.7
6.6.58	At Compton	1 mile	3:58 1
20.6.58	At Bakersfield: Heat of the U.S.A. 1 Mile Championship	1 mile	4:01.4
21.6.58	ditto. Final of same race	1 mile	3:57.9

In England

12.7.58	English Championships (Lost to Hewson and Rawson)	880 yards	1:49
22.7.58	Empire Games, Cardiff: Final of	880 yards	1:49.3
26.7.58	ditto	1 mile	3:59
4.8.58	London, White City: Empire v. Great Britain	880 yards	1:47.3
	(Fastest 880 yards and 800 metres for the European season. Third fastest 880 ever recorded)		
4.8.58	Watford (within two hours of above race)	880 yards	1:50.7
6.8.58	At Dublin, Eire (World record)	1 mile	3:54.5
7.8.58	ditto (next day)	2 mile	8:37.6
	(Second to Thomas who ran 8:32 for new World Record)		

In Sweden

25.8.58	At Stockholm	1,500 metres	3:41.7
28.8.58	At Gothenburg (World record)	1,500 metres	3:36
29.8.58	At Malmo	1 mile	3:58

In London

3.9.59	White City Stadium (The second fastest ever recorded)	1 mile	3:55.4

In Norway

5.9.58	In Oslo (The second fastest ever recorded)	1,500 metres	3:37.4

	Elliott had now recorded the two fastest miles and 1,500 metres ever run. He returned to Australia immediately after the Oslo race.		

Back in Australia

26.1.59	At Brisbane: Centennial Mile	1 mile	4:02.4
31.1.59	At Melbourne: Victorian Championships (Final)	880 yards	1:51 6
1.2.59	At Sydney: 4x1 Mile Relay (last leg)	1 mile	4:03.4
21.2.59	At Sydney	1 mile	4:07.2

Aged 21 years

4.3.59	At Melbourne	1,000 metres	2:25.3
9.3.59	At Melbourne: Moomba Carnival	1 mile	4:04.1
14.3.59	At Brisbane	1 mile	3:58.6
22.3.59	At Melbourne: 4x1 Mile Relay (last leg)	1 mile	4:04.6
	(A world record of 16:25.6 was set for this relay. The other runners were D. Wilson, A. Thomas, J. Murray)		
28.3.59	At Geraldton: West Australia (handicap)	3/4 mile	3:01.6

NOTE:

Elliott made a number of exhibition appearances that could hardly be called races. This was because of the demands made upon him that the public should see him in action.

Elliott only made these under duress, that is to keep faith with promoters of charitable organizations, etc.

Indeed, worn out by these and other public appearances he was unable to train or fit himself for his tasks.

Thus a very great career was spoilt by his latter races being run merely to win.

It is notable that even under these circumstances he was able to beat all opposition in Australia. The above list does not record all these appearances: only the more notable.

It is also notable that in scratch races he has never been beaten in the mile: and has only suffered defeat at all on three occasions.

It is my opinion that Herb Elliott, under propitious athletic conditions, could be expected to race faster as he becomes mature.

Also he could be expected to extend the distance of his events. That he could be expected to race very fast over distances up to six miles is shown by the fact that he holds the best times run at Portsea for repetitive runs up the sandhill and on the Hall Circuit: the first involving upwards of thirty minutes unremitting effort: the second approximately ten miles run around fifty-three minutes.

No other athlete has approached either of these efforts at Elliott's speed. It will be tragic for athletics if Elliott's studies, and his obligations involved in earning a livelihood, prevent the development of his full powers and possibilities.

A general commentary on Herb Elliott's running career, with special reference to certain races

(Written May 1959)

In Australia there are no Australian junior championships but State junior championships are held in conjunction with the Australian titles and are nominally the national junior titles. I understand this anomalous state of affairs is being amended. [Australian junior championships are now held every year. – Publisher]

In these two races in February 1955 Herb became national junior title holder for the 880 and one mile. No junior of promise was missing from either event.

Elliott won each event narrowly after being passed in the straight by older and better performed athletes.

He had taken over the lead going into the straight in each race, only to be passed by the athletes expected to win: in the case of the mile, Ron Clarke, afterwards to go on to run the world junior mile record at 4:06.8, and in the 880 yards by Doug Henderson, a 'Cerutty'-trained junior who had the current best times in Australia for a junior half-miler.

In these two races Elliott, who was junior in age to both these athletes, although apparently passed and beaten, showed his determination, will to win, and ability to 'drop and quicken', and thus snatch victory.

The first race I saw Herb Elliott run in in his native State of Western Australia was that on October 22, 1955.

On a rough grass track like a badly kept football ground or field, I was amazed to see the lad run 4:26 virtually as a solo effort, since no other schoolboy in the race was within 'cooee' of him. I then made the prediction, accepted without real belief, that 'within three years this lad could run the four-minute mile'.

The race, on February 20, 1957, was another race run on a football field, rough and as far removed from a good grass track as I have ever seen.

Unexpectedly Herb found, at the last minute, that the redoubtable Ron Clarke had been invited to run against him.

The race resulted in 4:04.4 being run for a new junior world record (Herb already held the record with 4:06 dead).

With two laps to go of the five-lap track, Herb took over from Clarke and decimated the field: the first of his really spectacular wins.

Herb started in the three-mile event on February 23, 1957, merely to set a new Australian junior 3,000 metres record, his last chance to set junior times as he turned nineteen years of age two days later.

In this race Geoff Warren, holder of the Australian three-mile record, not knowing the possibilities of the unknown Elliott as a three-miler, 'cleared out' from the gun, and at two miles had established a lead of some 100 yards over Elliott.

Having safely run his 3,000 metres record to the predetermined time schedule I had set him, Herb set out after Warren and considerably reduced his lead. In the circumstances, Herb's 'defeat' was a Pyrrhic loss: but it gave evidence of things to come.

In the three-mile, again on a country football field, on October 13 of the same year, a track marked out on a field that the night before was flooded from a cloud burst was muddy and generally as far from being a perfect running track as one could imagine: again Herb decimated the field, almost lapping Clarke who was predicted by the 'papers' to win, and soundly beating, amongst other crack three-milers, Neil Robbins, finalist in the Olympic Games 3,000 metres steeplechase, only the previous year. The time again was excellent under the conditions.

Despite the excellence of Herb's performances, no one, except those close to him, anticipated that he could hope to beat Merv Lincoln, who, it was confidently predicted, was the logical successor to Landy in the Australian realm of miling.

So the meeting between the tyro, ten days over nineteen years, with a best of 4:04.4, with the mature well-performed Olympic Games 1,500 metres finalist, was awaited with great interest, even with foregone conclusions as to the result being in favour of Lincoln.

The shock win of Elliott, who passed Lincoln in the back straight and went on to win in decisive fashion, was but the first of many more decisive wins over this great Australian miler.

At the time of writing Lincoln has yet to achieve his first victory over Elliott. Indeed, no man has ever defeated Elliott as a junior or senior over the mile.

His win over Lincoln in Perth in February 1958 was his closest call to a defeat.

Believing he had the race well won, he was surprised to find himself, with thirty yards to go, passed by a faster-finishing Lincoln. However, Elliott was able to 'drop', accelerate and snatch a narrow win. This was the one and only occasion Lincoln has been able to head Elliott once he has 'started out for home'. Indeed, no runner has ever passed Elliott once he has 'taken over and taken the lead.

In his defeat by Hewson in the 880, as is described, Herb endeavoured to lead all the way in a desperate attempt to steal the race from the start.

Elliott did not always set out to run the mile fast. At Brisbane, in the Australian Mile Championship, he decided to trail Lincoln – to reverse the usual procedure.

It was an unusual spectacle to see two of the world's greatest milers running last and second last in a mediocre field.

But again, with 600 yards to go, Elliott ran to the front, cut loose in the fastest last 440 yards ever run, to again win easily in the slow time of 4:08.8.

It was now evident, no matter how the race was run – fast, slow, in front, from the back of the field – no one in Australia could hope to defeat this twenty year old sand dune and hill-trained athlete.

No wonder the Americans were avid to see him, and invited me to travel with him at really luxurious expenses. But certain action taken by the over-enthusiastic amateur officials in Australia spoilt the trip for Herb.

The upsets would have completely discouraged anyone else but Herb Elliott.

His wonderful temperament rose superior to the situation. Again, the mark of the great champion.

However, had the track, a dirt and grass one prepared on the Coliseum Stadium at Los Angeles, not had a slow patch that, to me, obviously slowed Herb; and had he not suffered the official setbacks he did, a new world's record would have come out of the race, his first, in the U.S.A.

As it was, this great trier, said by our papers not to have the experience to win – the race was to go to Lincoln – ran only a few yards short of Ibbotson's unratified world record, and beat the official world record held by Landy who had run 3:57.9. Herb recorded 3:57.8.

The race at Compton, against the Irish-American champion Ron Delaney, winner of the Melbourne Olympic

Games 1,500 metres race in record time was to be the highlight of the tour. And so it was.

Before a crowded stadium sold out two weeks before the meet, the champions met. Ronnie was keen. Out on the track an hour before the event was due to start, he warmed up incessantly. Herb arrived only in reasonable time for his race, waited in the dressing room, and merely 'stretched' himself with a few preliminary runs of a hundred yards or so.

Then the race was on. It was obvious that it was to be a race of giants.

Delaney abandoned his usual sitting in at the back of the field tactics and kept close to Herb.

As my boy moved up to take over the lead in the third lap Ron was right on his heels. Then the débâcle came.

Ronnie struggled gamely to keep up, but before the bell lap was entered it was obvious, at least to me, that the race was over. And so it proved.

Down the back straight a tired Delaney gave in, to be beaten by eighty yards. Tabori, second, led the tired field home with Delaney third. No American-born athlete even looked like a challenge to the Australian. The time, 3:58.1, indicates that the early speed should have suited Delaney.

Elliott came up for his last race in America very, very tired. He had been away sightseeing for the two weeks prior to his race. Little or no training: much travel: many late nights. That is Herb's way. I was very definitely worried.

Nevertheless, I sent Herb out to keep his sub-four minute mile record intact as much as possible. People came to see just that.

A very tired Elliott failed in his heat to run the four minutes by one second.

A very much more tired – if it was possible – Elliott set out next day to run in the final. His most doughty opponent was Lincoln: Delaney missed the championships – he had gone home to Ireland.

Lincoln realized Herb was tired. Never had one man set out to beat another, unless it was Bannister to beat Landy, more than did Lincoln that night in Bakersfield, U.S.A.

But Herb was invincible. Tired as he was he flogged himself along in front: flogged himself up the straight – and won. Again to equal the official world record of my other Australian, Landy.

After this race I knew that in the right setting, a good fast early pace, Herb Elliott could lower the world record, not by tenths, but by seconds. And so it proved.

Over in England Herb set about seeing the sights: flying gliders, even riding bikes. He took his engagements before the Empire Games very lightly and suffered one of his few defeats. Hewson beat him in an 880 at White City. Yet Herb was able to run 1:49.

Tired out before his race he actually fell asleep on the floor of the dressing room.

Knowing he was not at his top he confided in me that his only chance was to clear out and lead from the gun – from start to finish. I let him go. No better tactics could be calculated to serve the interests of the usual waiting tactics adopted by English runners when against dangerous opponents.

Not only did Hewson sweep past a very tired Elliott coming up the straight – to go on to win handsomely, but Herb was also passed by another great English runner, Mike Rawson. It taught Herb a lesson.

For the Games 880 yards Herb settled down to some training. Against all predictions, he won a great tactical race: Herb was the master. The time was poorish, 1:49.3.

The mile at the Games was another débâcle, for all except the Australians. They ran first, second, third. And only Herb under the four minutes.

Back to the White City stadium after the Games. Herb was fit. He revenged himself on Hewson in no mean fashion, running the fastest 880 of the year: the third fastest ever, and of course, won. His time? 1:47.3.

Then the news from Australia. I saw the cable. Elliott not to run in Europe. However, after much interviewing, cabling and advising of our A.A.U., the order was rescinded. Herb could run but was not to be allowed expenses. Not even a fare or a car ride that could be construed as these dreadful expenses. Nevertheless the hospitality, the goodwill and friendship of our friends in Scandinavia won the day. Herb ran, and often.

The first race was a 1,500 metres two days after the finish of the European championships. Hewson had brilliantly won the European Championship 1,500 metres. Herb came out at a small meet and ran what was more or less an exhibition 1,500 metres, in a time one fifth of a second faster than the championship.

The Swedes, amongst the world's most knowledgeable and keen track fans, did not need to be told Herb was a real star.

It is true that, before coming to Sweden, where I had gone to see the championships, renew old friendships (we had travelled for a month to meets racing after Helsinki, in 1952) and especially to meet my old friend Gosta Holmer, to whom the world owed so much for his development of Fartlek, still the best method of conditioning runners.

As I say, the Swedes well knew Elliott had beaten the world record for the mile by some three seconds at Dublin. Only to confirm my own expressed public opinion, 'Elliott can run the mile in 3:55.' He proved me wrong by 0.5 of a second, on the right side!

So it is not surprising that when Elliott came up for his first 'big' race, at the Gothenburg stadium, the place was a sell out, and set a new attendance record for an athletic meeting in Sweden.

In the classiest 1,500 metre field ever assembled in one race, including the holder of the record, the gifted Jungwirth, still running at his top, Elliott made the field look like second-bests, won easily by some 25 metres (over 27 yards) and beat the record, which had been considered fantastic when Stanislav Jungwirth had set it, by more than two seconds.

Elliott was now big news: sought after: described in most flattering terms. To me, he was still a young Australian: strong, courageous to a fault, dedicated to his training, a believer in his coach. And above all, not daunted by times or reputations. Both of which are the greatest hurdles an athlete or coach has to surmount. Herb took both in his stride: casually, even.

He was rushed to White City, expenses or no expenses. He raced over the mile to another huge crowd. The second fastest mile ever recorded came up, less than a second slower than his own Dublin record, and nearly two seconds faster than the official record of Derek Ibbotson.

Back to Scandinavia, Herb ran his last European race. He was showing tiredness. This was to be his last race in Europe. Desperate attempts, by promoters, were made to get him to race in Finland. But as I crouched beside the track, minutely watching every sign as Herb raced past me – I could have touched him – I saw the signs of strain: that Herb was running on his will: I knew it was the end, at least for this season.

When he passed the tape, having run, again, inside the world record for 1,500 metres, I ran up him. His face, drawn and white, showed me he had 'had' it, as we Australians say. I said, 'Herb, that is your last race; you are going back to Australia.' Herb replied, 'I know,' meaning that he realized it, also. It was the end.

It is a pity more athletes and coaches do not realize when it is 'the end', for any season, or series of races. Too many, seeking those illusive ends associated with athletics, continue to race. They risk never racing at their top again. Something is done to their mentality: spirit. I have seen it too often. It is important to know when we are ready to race, superlatively. It is even more important to know when to stop.

Back in Australia Herb was lionized, and subjected to all the customary publicity that flatters the flatterers more than the one flattered.

Amongst other things conferred upon Herb was one of real value: a University scholarship. But the terms of the scholarship precluded the possibility of Herb's athletic advancement.

To gain admission to the English university for which the scholarship was awarded, Herb had to make good certain scholastic omissions in his education. No man can serve two masters. So running went into the discard: education and security became uppermost in Herb's life.

He decided to marry a school-time sweetheart. With little or no time to train, Herb proved that an athlete retains his form for much longer than the many think possible.

At Brisbane, before which he had expressed the serious opinion that he felt incapable of better than 4:20 for the mile, he recorded 4:02.4.

A week later ran in a relay 4:03.4; a few weeks later, March 9, 1959, ran a 4:04.1. All this with no training to speak of: in between a trip to the U.S.A. to receive 'awards', and trips around Australia for the same dubious reasons.

Five days later he was again in Brisbane and ran 3:58.6, truly the most amazing run of his career: worn out: untrained: insufficient rest, the champion was able to run one of the world's fastest miles on a grass track prepared on a cricket field.

So it was, for the track period of 1959, Herb Elliott ran eleven races. All these races were run by an athlete worn out by work, studies and travel. Little or no time to rest: little or no time to train.

Herb responded to the many demands made upon him by the unthinking people who see in him their own publicity ends, their turnstile-turning ends, and little of what the athlete has to endure: the strains and difficulties imposed upon him in the sacred name of sport.

Many of these races were purely exhibition runs, some

over the 3/4-mile distance, merely that the curious could see the champion in action. It is regrettable that such runs can be included in the list of recorded races of the champion. It is even more regrettable that talent such as Herb has developed to, and demonstrates, should be so lost to the world of good-fellowship, understanding and sportsmanship because of archaic rules.

Elliott, and those like him, are amongst the world's greatest ambassadors in the international realm. Maybe this is not considered desirable, or maybe it is only stodgy conservatism in high amateur circles.

To me, it will be truly calamitous if it so proves that the pressures, both economic and amateur, that he is subject to, stultify the career of one of the greatest athletes Australia and the world have thrown up.

He is only twenty-one years of age as I write. A career hardly started on. A maturity not even attained to. A promise, at his age, and for his distances, the world has never ever previously seen. May never see again. To me, it is an international situation. I hope it can be resolved, in the name of Sport, Athleticism, the ideals of the Olympic Games: for international understanding and goodwill. It could be so.

Don Keane

Don Keane, who practised in his walking the ideas and tenets that made Portsea runners supreme in Australia, with, perhaps, odd exceptions. A national champion at the very early age of twenty years, he achieved his successes too early and tended to lose incentive, and thus failed to fulfil in the world record field the promise shown in Australia.

Mike Agostini

Mike Agostini, who visited Australia in 1959 to race in Victoria and study the methods as taught at Portsea. However, running engagements abroad made it imperative that Mike leave Australia before he could be expected to completely assimilate our techniques.

In this picture, finishing without the stresses and strains set up by close finishes, Agostini crosses the line in perfect form, nicely relaxed, although having completed one of the fastest 220 yard races of his career.

Herb Elliott

Competing in the word record 4 x 1 mile relay in Melbourne, Herb shows what few runners show, a total absence of unnecessary shoulder sway. The steady shoulders, as the steady hips upon which the limbs swing independently, are two of my most adamant teachings. Nothing to me indicates poorer coaching than when I see a runner whose shoulder sway, and the swaying movement, apparently, initiating the arm movement, as it does. In extreme cases this produces many unnatural and grotesque styles that surely have nothing in common with grace, beauty, rhythm, power and, let it be said, world records.

In the past it may have been possible for world records to have been set, but the efficiency demanded today at the speeds athletes run at makes it evident to me that knowledge of, and attention to, technique is the main factor in world class coaching today. Unless the arms bend at the elbows it is impossible for any athlete to run without shoulder sway. The movement may be only that of an inch but it must be there.

APPENDIX II

Conditioning and training for various events

Sprinters

It is my opinion that the sprinters of the future, much more than in the past, will be expected to run the 400 metres (440 yards) event as well as the recognized 'dashes'.

It is also my opinion that when a sprinter is properly conditioned and trained to run a fast 440, rather than losing speed for the shorter events, he should be faster. The reason being that conditioning for greater stamina and strength should make it possible to draw on greater ability for the shorter distances.

Sprinting, however, calls on so little need for prolonged training that the sprint athlete is best adopting another sport for the six months of the 'off' season. Any sport or activity that makes for agility and speed so long as not too dangerous or subjecting the athlete to serious leg injuries.

Hockey immediately suggests itself. Lacrosse, tennis, basket-ball, and similar sports must keep an athlete fit and interested in activity. Gymnastics would be a 'must', and if he is really keen he will undertake regular cross country runs of three to five miles, once or twice a week.

He will also do running on the spot at terrific speed in the gym or indoor hall if the climate is too inclement to work outdoors. Nothing is better for strength-gaining than hill – and/or sandhill running in this period: always done at the fastest speeds possible.

The sprinter, in particular, must never train too easily. His events require speed above all else. He must practise speed: dynamic movement as much as possible. The greatest need for all athletes is strength. More and more strength. It is entirely fallacious to say that acquired strength makes the athlete sluggish. Greater strength, properly acquired by fast movements as is required by the weight-lifter cleaning a heavy weight, makes for faster, stronger, more dynamic effort when the strength is used in running.

However, it is technique, rather than what to do, that is of fundamental importance, and if the sprinter has not the 'clues' how, to run all the training is little likely to improve him: could quite conceivably make his chance of being a great sprinter worse than heretofore.

So it is important for the young sprinter to get real evidence that his speed is improving. Then he will know that what he is doing is reasonably correct. The objective of training is to improve, and continued training to continue to improve. Obviously there must be a point, or speed, above which each individual cannot pass.

Once race practice commences, the sprinter must visit the track on three days, and much of his work, of necessity, must be in short dashes in which he strives with all the power of his personality, rather than the brute strength of his physical body, to move over the ground faster and faster, more and more efficiently.

I believe this can be practised best in wind sprints rather than in bursts up the sprint track. Such bursts, by a conditioned reflex, only too often seem to train an athlete to burst out of the blocks, run at high speed for thirty or forty yards, and then ease up and repeat the performances.

I favour an orthodox starting position with the feet fairly wide apart, that is the knee of the back foot somewhere near the position of the front foot when on the mark position. There should be a slight inclination upwards from the rear to the shoulders, if the relation of the legs to the trunk permits of this.

The weight of the body rests lightly on the outstretched fingers, and is held poised and steady by focussing the attention on a spot on the track where the rear foot can be expected to fall in its first stride. On no account, once the set position is adopted, should the athlete look up the track. This causes loss of concentration and the body tends to rock. No athlete who knows how to concentrate on his start in the manner that I have described will ever 'break', unless, of course, he does so deliberately in attempting to anticipate the gun.

The body goes out like a bullet and on the same trajectory. I have measured Hogan and it will take as much as thirty yards before he has assumed his normal upright running posture. At that distance I have never seen him headed in a normal start. But to go on from there against the world's greatest proved to be Hec Hogan's difficulty.

So the sprinter will practise flat-out efforts over the various parts of his track. That means he will often practise racing within himself to a spot approximating one-third of his race distance; from there to the two-thirds spot he will endeavour to run in an all-out effort. He will practise running to the two-thirds spot, and finishing to the finish and ten yards beyond in the same all-out effort. Thus he will have a chance of conditioning his reflexes to running his event in a series of fast surges at his very top effort.

All races up to the 440 yards can be practised in this manner. In other respects the practices of sprinters are too well known to need repetition. Really fast men are born. But all can hope for some improvement.

A week's workout, in the conditioning period, for those who have the time and opportunities, could be:

In each week: Two runs across country from three miles to five miles.

One session at gymnastics, say one hour's duration. Two sessions of heavy weight-resistance exercises each of one hour; possibly three sessions.

An hour's practice at some extra sport.

Two hours' participation in a game involving this sport.

Some daily practice, from fifteen to thirty minutes practising fast running on the spot, or short bursts following running on the spot either outside or inside.

Each day some dynamic movements that simulate sprint running, and an easy run from 880 yards to one mile.

In the Race Practice Period: the two or three months before actual competition.

Each week: Two visits to the track to practise what has been suggested in the text: viz, starting, wind sprinting, sectional speed practice of the event(s): some run-throughs.

Two twenty-minute to thirty-minute sessions with heavy weights.

One run from one mile to three miles.

Some practice and an afternoon's sport at some other activity.

One hour's gymnastics, rope-climbing, etc.

Daily, some spot-running: stride-stretching; limbering exercises.

Competition: Two or three times each week.

Other days: Some starting, flat out efforts over various parts of the events distances. Every day: some dynamic movements: running on the spot and limbering exercises. Run throughs.

440 yards to 880 yards

Conditioning: (six months). Each week: average of twenty to forty miles. All efforts want to be hard and powerful: easing down only sufficiently for the recovery to permit of the work continuing.

Each week: Two hard sessions of at least one hour's duration with heavy weights, possibly three.

At least three long runs of five miles in less than thirty minutes and two or three runs of from one to three miles. These can be run steadily or intermittently, in any case variety of speed and the distance run in the fast bursts must be constantly varied.

- One session of gymnastics: one session sandhill or similar. Occasionally, say once a month, a run up to ten miles cross country.

Race Practice: approximately three months.

The golf links and parks are ideal for the varying speed work that is the main part of race practice. This work can be done for a minimum of one hour and the intensity will vary with the type and ability of each athlete. If the work can be continued for two hours it has been done at too easy speeds, although the stronger types will always be able to do more work, and recover better than weaker types.

Occasional visits to grass tracks for the purpose of speed checkups are O.K. But if nothing more than flat running is engaged in there is little likelihood of real power and strength being developed.

The undulating courses make for the acquiring of speed when the down slopes are used for flat-out running, and up grades make for the ability to bring in the whole of the drive as when an athlete surges away from his competitors, or accelerates in the straight.

The ability to accelerate at will: to 'take off' and surge: all these aspects of racing need unremitting practice.

Approximately half of the race practice time should be occupied by practising at the pre-determined speeds the athlete wishes to race at: varying these speeds as he practises for his specialized event or other events. However this may be he will do most of the speed running at the event speed, events requiring either faster or slower speeds looking after themselves and not requiring any other than occasional practice.

The distances that the racing speed is held will constantly vary from thirty to forty yards to 300 and 350 yards in the case of the 440; and from sixty to eighty-yard bursts to 660 and 700 yards in the case of the 880. Occasionally over distance hard efforts can be done.

The other general 50 per cent of race practice will be done

by holding a hard and testing effort for the duration of time that is aimed at. Suppose it is forty-seven seconds in the case of the 440, quite a number of efforts will be run, and repeated, not at the speed of forty-seven seconds for 440, since that would be impossible or most unlikely. If it was possible then the aim or pre-determined speed is too low. But the effort will be 'almost but not quite' and will be held for around forty-five to fifty seconds. Or around 1:50 plus or minus five seconds in the case of fast half-mile aspirants.

In this way the organism gets conditioned to two things: moving at a certain pre-determined speed: holding a hard effort for a predetermined time. What these efforts and times are each must determine for himself.

Obviously, what these pre-determined speeds will be must be related to the age, experience and ability of each athlete.

When racing commences then, little or no training is done to improve the standard of ability that has been arrived at. It is useless to expect to expend substantially and to accrue substantially at one and the same time. However, if the racing is weekly, even if oftener, enough high-pressure effort of short duration is needed to keep tuned up to top racing fitness. Only the athlete can learn for himself what is required. Certainly it must not be exhaustive.

Sometimes a hard work-out maybe called for, but the usual thing is for most athletes to over-train between races. Of course, the athlete who is not prepared and conditioned with a long and sincere background desperately tries to make amends by hard efforts in the racing period. But he can hardly hope to succeed if his object is to run world-class times.

The club athlete, those who play around with their sport on a Saturday, and mostly forget it during the week, or only seriously train when in sight of the Track Season, such an athlete is hardly likely to read these hints, much less obtain any real benefit from what is suggested.

Yet any athlete who can experiment for himself, test, try,

and adapt these principles, should show an improvement in his performances; even if not an immediate one. The principles have been well tried out in Australia.

880 yards – 1 mile

Conditioning: Six months. Each week an average of forty to fifty miles per week. This work is also done hard and with power.

Each week: Some sandhill work if possible. Or other hill work. If very severe this is done repetitively with rests until it can be continuous, with only easing down to rest on the downhill section.

The 880 – 1 mile type, being slower than the 440 – 880 type, will compensate for this slower speed by longer distance.

Not that the speed is everything: it is the technique and the quality of the effort, that is important. Plenty of long intermittently hard or steady running each day, or most days, some, even when the customary weight-resistance sessions are done. These sessions, as those of gymnastics, will be taken incidentally, as it were. Some running can be done somewhere in the day on most days.

All types and events are benefited by occasional long hard walks in the mountains, sand-running occasionally, and very occasionally, say, twice in the season, a twenty-miler, run very hard.

Race Practice: Three months. This will be similar to the 440 – 880 athletes' practice except that it will be much more extensive, and according to type, from twenty to forty miles per week.

The customary golf–link work: the visit, perhaps twice in the week, to the grass track: the continuous attempt to train the organism to surge, accelerate, pass competitors, until all these factors for success become instinctive.

This athlete will also, in a general way, direct one-half of his training effort to inuring his body to the speed at which it is to travel, and for the length of time that it has to hold extreme and punishing effort.

This is a basic part of our methods, as it is to practise surging, passing and overtaking. In a word the continual varying of pace. Top-flight racing of the future, and this has already become fact, is no longer run at steady paces. Once the race has settled down, say after the first lap in a mile race, the pace of the race should fluctuate.

Always some runner should be varying the pace, surging into the lead: dropping back: but in principle testing out, breaking up, responding to the cyclic beats, pulsing and surges that are more increasingly being recognized as the art of running.

Zatopek was the first of the greats to introduce these variations into his running, and in his day, with outstanding success.

The idea that a constantly held speed is the most economical pace is not true. Energy comes in bursts and should be availed of as it comes. This is not to suggest that a miler tears away at some breakneck pace: then drops almost to a walk and when recovered tears away again for a sprint-like burst: nothing could be more ridiculous. But it does suggest that energy ebbs and flows: that the zombie-like, almost static movements that we see so often will never produce the records of the future, no matter what may have been produced in the past.

As with shorter events, once racing commences little or no attempt is made to improve in the strength available: but every effort can be made to translate the strength accumulated, built-in, and the practice that has been done be released in fast racing.

The concentration (excitement) that is aroused by important events should be sufficient to release emotionally the in-built energy. If it is not there no emotion can bring out what isn't there. But lack of vital interest, lack of emotional stimulus, staleness, these things can fail to release energy that may be locked up in the organism: or what we often find, fail to drain the organism of all but the last dregs.

Some exercise, each or every other day, may be called for once racing commences.

But it should stop short of being too exhausting: definitely. More races are lost on the track than lost through insufficient training during the racing period.

Indeed, some athletes perform with little or no training once they start racing, although I, myself; prefer some exercise most days. It all depends on the individual athlete: his particular personality. Each athlete and each coach must determine these things for himself.

I find the apparent answers come along: the correct action seems to suggest itself. Experience here, and an instinctive response based in it, rather than an intellectual determination based on it, seems to be the factor.

Personally, I find the greatest difficulty in generalizing so that I meet the need of a particular athlete.

My own system involves getting to know each athlete in all departments of his personality.

Until I get to know him I feel I can only roughly guess as to how much work he can take: what punishment will or will not break him down, make him a plodder, and each situation is evaluated and decided on its merits, on the day, according to the need of the moment. If the coach cannot come to grips with each athlete, completely and intimately, he must resort to guessing as to the athlete's needs: or the athlete find out his own needs.

1 mile – 3 miles

Conditioning: as all other events: Six months: fifty to sixty miles per week.

As with the 880 – 1 mile conditioning, there will be similar periods or sessions devoted to strength work with heavy weights and resistance: some gymnasium or similar work: and when able to do so, long and hard walks in mountains, or across deserts. In a word all those things that tend to appeal and find a response in those destined to be great in something.

As I have said, championship is a state of mind – first. And the great are born to their destiny. This may not be very satisfactory for those 'triers' who need a concise primer: a detailed blue-print.

And I must reiterate that success does not lie in any such things. The ease with which schedules can be written, the demand for them, and the readiness of certain types of coaches to supply them – I can only say, if it was that easy, any successful coach could make a fortune. Indeed, some would appear to do so. And no doubt many mediocre athletes gain some advantage.

But I encourage the athlete to reach a stage where he can be his own trainer – mostly – self-determining as to what he should do. Sufficient is that he has some approximation of what constitutes a week's conditioning, a week's race practice, and some hints on in between racing training.

The one mile-three mile type, of which Albert Thomas is typical, will find, without specially doing conditioning for the mile or the six mile events, that his specialization in the three mile will result, as it has for Thomas, in him running close to world bests in both the mile and six if he succeeds in running a world record for the three.

Iharos would be another case in point. When well conditioned the athlete can set world records above and below his specialization. Zatopek would be an even better illustration, perhaps.

So, we work mainly with the idea of accustoming the organism to move at optimum speeds for the event that seems to suggest optimum success. And we work in the various ways suggested to help the body build up the type of organism that makes what we aim at of reasonable attainment.

Race practice: This also is similar in principle to all that has been stated in regard to the other events. But the three-miler must be able to hold his high speeds for as long as 14 minutes – for the 5,000 metres. So he will run at good and hard speeds up to fifteen minutes and then maybe, ease down, but never to walking, and when sufficiently recovered subject his organism to another dose, and as long as it can take it. This may be for an hour and one half. But it must not be continued at slow laborious levels.

It is in such practice that, with occasional steady runs up to six, eight or ten miles, the three-miler finds he has developed good six-mile ability. Also his practice, where he 'takes'-off in hard fast bursts of various distances from eighty yards to 880 yards, that he has acquired the ability to run commensurately fast miles.

Once racing commences, the athlete who runs three milers needs to watch that he does not exhaust himself with too long runs between races. A hard ten-mile run can exhaust an athlete for as long as three days. However, the athlete will feel his own powers, or lack of them. And when experienced can be left to make his own determinations.

When properly conditioned such athletes will find they can race at their top on two successive days: or as much as three times in a week.

Always providing they get sufficient rest, but not necessarily sleep. The physical body, in adults, needs physical rest more than long hours of sleep. This rest can be taken in airplanes, trains, etc.; in cat-naps as well as in bed. Also the athlete is advised to go to bed when he can, irrespective of the hour of day, if that is the only time he can get proper rest in bed.

Too many imagine they must be weak because they have travelled all night. A little reflection will show that nothing is usually done to drain the body of energy: that the feeling is usually a lethargic one due to the boredom of travel. On the other hand, an athlete who has been walking all day sight-seeing, or spent his usual hours of rest dancing in a night club, or emotionally exhausting himself in erotic adventures, is little likely to find his reservoir of physical energy brimming over.

In any case two or three days' quiet in some set-up such as

one finds in Sweden – sporting holiday resorts specially catering for athletes at very moderate rates, or any country or seaside resort that is quiet and restful – can be calculated to restore the athlete.

It is remarkable the recovery that can be made in a week when the organism is conditioned to the work. Otherwise a breakdown can mean no more racing for six or more months.

Conditioning over the years does not necessarily mean faster and faster times. It can do so, of course.

But it makes for almost a complete recovery from exhaustive efforts, often in minutes: and the ability to come up for repeated exhaustive efforts.

3 mile – 6 mile

Conditioning: This follows on the same lines as the one mile – three mile suggestions. Each week some weight work designed to make it possible that the athlete can lift his body-weight overhead, etc.

But the six-miler type will be a six-miler because he has found greater success in the longer distances.

He will tend to run normally at slower speeds. Therefore his distances in training will be longer to compensate for the lesser effort as expressed in speed.

It should be recognized that all running is merely shifting the bodyweight from one spot to another: that the faster we do this given equal technique, the more exhaustive is the effort. Some types seem incapable of releasing all their energy in short fast bursts. They are recognized as 'stamina' types.

To develop this stamina to a high degree requires more actual miles in running than when speed is a bigger factor than stamina. Therefore the three to six-miler type will need to reconcile himself to a very high mileage per week. He will move up to as high as 100 per week, some weeks.

This is not high when one considers that at the slightly slower rates, spread over three sessions in a day as is possible, in week-ends, a total of sixty miles can be built up for the two days on occasion. For him, as he works up to world class, it will be run and rest. An average of ten miles a day for the other three or four days is not out of the way, with gym work and lifting extra.

In this I have in mind those who would hope to run the world records of the future. Athletes are increasingly devoting themselves to a partial full-time attempt to reach the top. I say partial since it is not essential to abandon other work all the time, but it is essential to take time off from the usual daily avocation to do the necessary build-up unless one is prepared to take years to get where they might get in months, physically.

Long runs in the mountains up to twenty miles: almost the same distances occasionally on the heavy beach sands are the means that seem to have proved efficacious in the past, and may be considered to produce the faster racing of the future.

In these events, strength, as in all events, is the deciding factor, today. I find that a lad who can only run the sandhill six repetitions, although he may be able to outsprint a six-miler, is far less likely to run a fast mile, or, event for event, succeed on as high a level.

I find the same on the Hall Circuit, that 1 mile 283 yards of strenuous Fartlek, where those who can run it fast, and continue running it fast up to eight or ten laps are the ones who will run faster over the mile as well as acquit themselves well up to six miles.

Strength comes only through the breaking down of muscle tissue consistently undertaken. Speed comes from using that strength efficiently within the type and compass of the personality. All we need to know is what we are 'born' to do. So, if an athlete realizes he has not the intrinsic ability to run at the fastest mile speeds and he extends his event to the three to six-mile field, he needs must do more miles to reach the same degree of exhaustion, and thereby benefit as his naturally better co-ordinated, quicker tempo co-athlete.

In his race training he will extend his efforts. A good six-miler today, or by my standards, needs to be able to pour out a fast mile in any part of his race if he scents victory from doing so.

This event now calls for the ability to be able to run under fourteen minutes as routine for three miles, and much practice must be done at speeds that correspond to this rate. Not, of course, maintaining the speed for three miles in training, but moving up to that rate and holding it for as long as possible, only easing down to recover enough to continue the work.

These rates are not so high as most think. It must no longer be considered that 440 yards run between sixty-five and seventy seconds is fast. It is true it takes strength to maintain such speeds and no effort must be spared to gain that strength so that the speeds can be held for a mile or two at will.

It is also necessary to realize that it is not necessary to be able to race at such speeds for, say, even four miles in training and yet on the right day in the right race find that one can race at equivalent speeds and hold them, even running faster for the full distance.

Whilst it is essential in my view to practise at the speed that one pre-determines, nevertheless the athlete can be expected to race at somewhat higher speeds than he may be able to hold in his race practice. For instance, the six-miler may find that holding a 4:40 mile rate for various distances almost beyond his ability in his training, yet find that he can race at the same speed quite successfully. Many athletes can allow from 5 per cent to 10 per cent increase in their speeds above what they can hold in training.

On the other hand high–speed running for all events should be practised at least one session each week. At Portsea we usually do this on one of the weekend sessions at noontime. Fast 110 yard and 220 yard speeds are done at the highest rates possible for each athlete.

The three – six miler must practise, as must all athletes, for all events, varying pace so that he can surge away at will in the race, pick-up speed instantly when a competitor passes at a fast speed, and condition himself to quicken at bell laps. The best men at these distances will also be able to hold a rate for a mile run in the six-mile considered to be at such a speed that the other competitors abandon the rate after a lap or two.

All this can be practised until such tactics become instinctive and normal.

Obviously it is not sensible to start doing these break-away tactics early in the race, especially if an athlete or athletes can be considered to be as strong, or faster and stronger. Unless an athlete can hope to maintain the race speed, and not be overtaken after a surge or burst, it is not sensible to waste his energy in such abortive tactics.

But if he can maintain the race pace, or even quicken it, as could Zatopek, then such tactics, properly employed, can be considered race winners, and produce, we hope, record runs.

As with all others the athlete who would run fast threes and sixes needs to conserve his energy once racing starts. An easy run up to six miles Fartlek in the country will help him keep good form for the three, and up to ten miles for the six. Some fast bursts at full racing speed over half a mile is all that is needed if the races occur once or twice a week. Three events in a week would require all the rest possible between them and no training at all.

The longer the race the more foolish it is to run so far to be beaten in the last few yards. The first class three – and six – specialist will endeavour to have his race won before he enters the last lap – if it is possible to do so.

The Marathon and Longer Distances

Conditioning: Today the athlete who is well conditioned for the six-mile event has proved to be even better fitted to race the marathon than the athlete who has concentrated solely on the longer distance. This is due to the fact that the six-miler trains at higher rates than the marathon man: his stamina work is sufficient to develop all the strength he needs to run the marathon distance: and possibly, being a six-miler – which means down to the mile – fast, also he is probably a better co-ordinated mover.

However as all this may be I definitely feel that many marathon men do far too much in mileage when they exceed 400 per month, and consequently far too little at the speeds that marathons are now run. I also have the speeds of the future in mind.

For a good, easy mover a speed of five minutes a mile does not seem excessive to me. It is the strength to be able to keep this rate up for twenty-six miles that is the difficulty. So anything that can make the marathon man over-all stronger as an organism must help him.

I feel, when we consider the times of the future, that running alone will not provide the answer. Running and more running will tend to make the marathon man into a fifty-miler or a 100-mile man.

Above 400 per month it would appear that the pace (rate per mile) has to be slowed down so much that the organism is not conditioned to the required speed.

In the beginning, the newcomer to the marathon is best running, and running, until he has mastered the ability to keep going for the full marathon distance. To give added confidence, he could well master running to thirty miles, knowing he can do so when he may have to.

Once he has acquired that ability he must concentrate on speed. He will pre-determine at what rate he hopes to race his marathon and will do a lot of his training at this speed. For example, assume it is the five-minute-per-mile rate. He will get his organism used to this speed by running repetitive three miles or five miles easing down between the efforts sufficiently to recover. If he can manage two or three such repetitive efforts he will have had a very good work-out.

His objective will be to be able to run ten miles in training in fifty minutes, and on occasion extend the distance at this rate to fifteen miles even if this is only accomplished in a race.

I must reiterate that the rate can be applied to each athlete according to his ability and ambition. It could be as low as seven minutes per mile, although I would suggest that any beginner, today, who is not capable of a better performance than a marathon run in three hours would be best advised to go away and make himself strong by hard mountain walking up to thirty miles per day, as well as a hard course of gymnastics and weight-training.

He could combine this with long runs at almost any pace up to thirty miles. When sufficient strength is built-in then such a one should be able to very soon run a marathon around the six-minute-per-mile rate.

Certainly better than a seven-minutes-per-mile pace. I hold this view because too many poor types get an easy ego-gratification by plodding in poor form and style over the marathon distance in what amounts to really poor times and performances that tend to make a burlesque of one of the toughest events in any sport any man can compete in.

Age, to me, is no excuse.

The aged, partly fit and similar, can do their running privately. There definitely should be a time limit on all events, especially that of the marathon.

A very generous limit of 3:30 is suggested, which is one hour fifteen minutes slower than the best times recorded.

This is equivalent to a man running in a mile race who is unable to run even a six-minute mile, and who would be labouring along in the third lap when the four-minute miler had run out the winner: an obviously ridiculous situation in mile running, but which is tolerated in marathon running, even championships. This is not an intolerant attitude but an appeal to place the event on a proper footing and to exclude the cranks and exhibitionists.

Little or no training would be done on the bitumen or concrete roads. I am one who does not believe that the body can ever get inured to running fast and with free movements if it is trained on hard artificial tracks and roads. It is bad enough that the athlete has to race on such mediums: to me another illustration of how far intellectual decisions made by officials differ profoundly from the conclusions arrived at by serious experimenters, and knowledgeable performers. It seemed to be overlooked that when road and marathon running was first recognized as a sport the events were run on sandy country roads quite different to the modern sealed motor road.

So the marathon man, meaning the road runner, must watch that his musculature does not respond by shortening his stride, and by the development of a restricted gait that almost completely inhibits the possibility of being a free mover, with commensurate high speeds.

It is so rare to find a marathon man that can run a mile in 4:15 that we have to turn to the six-miler who can do so, such as Power of Australia.

Peters of England developed on the right lines. He would run five or six miles fast during the day, and around ten miles hard of an evening. It would appear that this was the basis of his phenomenal times. Basically that is the form of training that I advocate.

However, I would suggest that the marathon man, as indeed all athletes, practise varying his pace so that he can whip in a fast mile at almost any stage of the race. To be able to do this takes practice and is not necessarily an act of will.

Also, he should practise surging: that ability to quicken for 440 yards, sink back to the common pace, and repeat it as often as the athlete desires to do so.

To run in this fashion mitigates against the treadmill one-pace that distance men in particular drift into.

The athlete who practises surging, and can do so at will, is still rare. But other things being equal he has a winner. But it takes constant practice. It is useless to talk about such things and then hope to put them into practice in a race. As we train so we race. And we shall race as we have trained.

It has also been my practice to advocate that the marathon man pays so much attention to detail that he will go out for a run, not necessarily any great distance, even five miles will do, and enter a sports ground and learn to race faster over the last quarter-mile. This is a 'conditioned response' – a factor upon which I place the greatest importance, after technique and strength.

How futile to have run twenty-six miles and then be beaten because one was unable by an effort of will to increase pace. The conditioned response makes such finishing efforts normal and automatic.

All athletes, irrespective of the distance of their events, are benefited by going to a grass track or a golf links, or similar, and learning to run very fast. Those who cannot run off a 220 in better than thirty seconds can hardly be expected to demonstrate much speed in bursts and surges.

Marathon runners, more than most, tend to develop into plodders: to go out and run as a kind of duty. It is good, therefore, to take a day's rest from training each week – Monday is usually the best day – and break the routine of daily running by a week or so occasionally doing long and arduous walks in mountains with heavy packs. In Australia, or rather this corner of it, there are ample high mountains around 6,000 feet and a walker can walk for hundreds of miles at elevations over 4,000 feet with no habitations. His pack will weigh upwards of forty pounds.

All athletes can do with a complete hibernation period of at least three days, especially in the winter time. During this time no work at all is engaged in, or training. The athlete will rest, read and sleep, moving around only as much as is needed to get his food, etc.

Such hibernations are excellent in some hut by the ocean

or in the mountains. We live in an environment that makes occasional hibernations normal. One rises from them like a giant refreshed.

Marathon running must now be considered as we once considered ten mile and fifteen mile events: a distance event, but one in which speed is a very definite factor. It is all a matter of concepts: stepped up training and added power (strength).

The Jumps, Field Games, etc.

I do not think that this book is the proper place to try and develop my many ideas on the various events in athletics other than running. But I do suggest that athletes interested in any and all events can be benefited by understanding proper posture and running movements: as well as being able to demonstrate them. Even in the run up of the discus, javelin, and particularly the jumps, long, high and hop step and jump.

Much is to be gained by running practice and the freeing movements that I advocate. And the development of greater strength and agility must augment the potential of all athletes.

The search for new approaches and variations of technique must go on ceaselessly. The athlete who waits for his coach to suggest all that he does is not likely to succeed on the highest levels. Indeed, all great athletes are innovators in their own right. Zatopek: O'Brien: such names immediately suggest themselves.

The gymnasium and the weight–lifting area will do more to advance performances than the ceaseless repetitive training that is so beloved of my field games exponents. These athletes tend to make much of small points in technique. They are often chagrined to find some rough novice, whose technique causes superior smiles, throws or heaves further.

Whilst technique is important, it is results that count. Strong men mostly outdo weaker types in everything. Nothing is worse, in my view, than big men throwing, with every evidence of mainly being big, rather than strong. But when both very big and very strong, then their power may well prove irresistible.

Dexterity and dynamic movement rest in strength, properly acquired, and as properly applied. In my opinion, generally speaking, neither have been particularly exploited. Techniques being equal, as they so often are, the difference in results can be expected to come from added strength. If not from this source, then what other?

For all events   hurdling, throwing, jumping   the factor most likely to produce the records of the future is strength   systematically acquired, and intelligently applied.

APPENDIX III

Some comments on record-breaking

It is entirely wrong for any athlete to consider that the be-all and end-all of racing is beating this one or that. It is not. Any athlete may beat a superior athlete who may be inferior to him on an odd occasion. It is ridiculous to get elated over such victories. Just as it is ridiculous for a champion to get inflated ego because he easily beats all or most of the opposition.

The time the race is won in, or the conditions it is won in as to heat (temperature), wind, and track conditions must be taken into account. We have all seen the athlete who sits in behind a pace maker(s) and then sprints to an easy win. Often such an athlete is the acknowledged champion of the race. His place, to me, is in front, if not for the whole of the race, at least from when the pace starts to hurt. I do not like the consistent sitter. He evidences a personality of a narrow type: is a natural 'user-upperer' as we call them. There is something of the parasitic in such tactics.

On the contrary, juniors, or those not acknowledged as the 'top' man, are perfectly justified to follow the pace of their 'betters'. If they are destined to be great they will set out to lead at the critical part of the race – if they can.

It is my policy, and always has been, to train my athletes to be front runners. The policy may not always succeed for all: but it imbues a confidence and manliness that the less venturesome can never know. Winning is not everything – if it implies using up others, or is gained by slowing-up tactics: blocking, and the like. We will have none of such things.

Every athlete, whilst he may hope to win, will gain more

from running fast especially if he can follow another over a record. Such a one will be very unfortunate if he, also, on his day, does not set a winning record. It is wrong to develop a complex about beating another competitor as if that was all that there was to the sport.

Such an approach is juvenile. It implies certain states that make it appear to win justifies some personal attitude or nationalistic one. I make a clear distinction between winning and excelling.

Excelling implies winning: but it also implies running very fast, record fast. Excelling implies giving proper value to the means whereby the winning takes place: beauty of technique, courageous effort, initiative, and finally, great speed.

To me it is of the greatest importance to concentrate on excelling in life rather than merely gaining. To have known oneself to have been the fastest man in the world for some event, no matter for how short a duration, is to me a far superior thing than boasting of the number of races one has won, or the athletes one has beaten.

The one can be meaningless if the competition is weak: the other implies a disregard for the feelings of the defeated. Every success and elation is a defeat and a sadness for someone else. But no one begrudges the athlete who sets a record his success. It is an honour, often, to have taken part in such an event since all contribute, in some way to such a success and a record.

Everyone can be a record-breaker. Not seeking out easy ones, or unusual ones that can be beaten, merely to boast of these things – but it is good to set about taking a club record: or a meet record: and so on up the scale. In my experience great happenings resulted from embarking upon such a project, and carrying it out to its possibilities. It ended, in Australia, in otherwise unknown athletes continuing their record-breaking careers until they ran new Australian times, and competed at Olympic Games, when more gifted types who in the first instance were race-winners, and only that, failed to go on, failed to find any real niche in the history of athletics in my country, Australia.

It is worth while to try and win, with all the resources we can muster, one of the great Games: Olympic, European, etc. But there is a modicum of chance in such events. Run over again it often would mean another would win. But when an athlete runs a world record – sets himself to do so – as I would set an athlete, then he can rest on the record until another wrests it from him, even as he wrested it from a predecessor.

One can be champion in some event in a year when the level of that event is not as high as it might be. It is hard to compare champions. It is relatively easy to compare world record-breakers.

Therefore we live in the day of the Statistician: the man who lists the distances, heights and speeds the athletes perform at. Today it is one's rating in the world that is important: not whom one has beaten: or the number of races won.

You may not like this: you may reject it: but the statistician has come to stay, and your position in the sphere of things is clear, that is, if you appear in his lists. Even clubs are now statistically minded and rank their athletes. They must do it when they choose teams anyway.

Long after we have forgotten who beat whom we will be poring over the lists of the great ones who ran record times. By their attitudes to these things do we know them.

It can be asked, must not the day arrive when it will be impossible to set new records: that the limits of speed and endurance will have been met. But I say that day is a very long way off: that man, by intensive effort and greater knowledge, can be expected to perform very much better than we have seen up to the present.

With only a few exceptions athletics has been generally considered something indulged in seriously by adolescents. Science has hardly bothered to consider the factors involved. The real field of activity is in the future rather than the past.

Even when science and full-time devotion has produced the limits that can be expected from humans, then athletes will be evaluated in terms of each year's efforts. It is no small thing to have run the world's fastest 800 metres for a given year, or jumped the highest that year in Europe, and so on.

Then we might move where other factors are considered as well as speed and distance. Such factors as beauty of movement and execution: whether the athlete led all the way in a race: what time intermediate sections of the race were run in: also the full personality may be taken into consideration, such as the intellectual status of the athlete, his artistic and aesthetic nature.

It must not be forgotten that the ancient Greeks, in their Olympic Games, demanded that wars ceased at the time of the Games, and that the athletes were expected to write odes, exhibit a perfection of grace and beauty, as well as perform on a purely physical basis.

At present development of modern man it is the physical rather than the aesthetic that is valued. The fact of winning rather than the art of excelling. However, the object of this book has been to suggest that the two may be combined.